# MONEY IN THEIR OWN NAME:
# THE FEMINIST VOICE IN POVERTY DEBATE
# IN CANADA, 1970–1995

In *Money in Their Own Name*, Wendy McKeen examines the relationship between gender and social policy in Canada from the 1970s to the 1990s. Providing a detailed historical account of the shaping of feminist politics within the field of federal child benefits programs in Canada, she explores the critical issue of why the feminist vision of the 'social individual' failed to flourish.

Canadian social policy has established women's access to social benefits on the basis of their status as wives or mothers, not as individuals in their own right. In her analysis, McKeen discusses this persistent familialism that has been written and rewritten into Canadian social policy, and shows how this approach reinforces women's dependency. She further demonstrates the lack of contest by the women's movement toward this dependent status, and the consequent erasure of women from social policy.

McKeen effectively weaves together sociological theory with concrete examples of political struggle. She uncovers overlooked aspects of Canadian social policy politics and subsequently extends our understanding of the political process. At the same time, by synthesizing the concepts of discourse, agency, and policy community, she offers a new analytical tool for understanding how the political interests of actors are shaped.

(Studies in Comparative Political Economy and Public Policy)

WENDY E. MCKEEN is an assistant professor at the Maritime School of Social Work at Dalhousie University.

## Studies in Comparative Political Economy and Public Pollicy

Editors: MICHAEL HOWLETT, DAVID LAYCOCK, STEPHEN McBRIDE,
Simon Fraser University.

*Studies in Comparative Political Economy and Public Policy* is designed
to showcase innovative approaches to political economy and public policy
from a comparative perspective. While originating in Canada, the series will
provide attractive offerings to a wide international audience, featuring studies
with local, subnational, cross-national, and international empirical bases and
theoretical frameworks.

*Editorial Advisory Board*

For a list of books published in the series, see p. 169.

# Money in Their Own Name

The Feminist Voice in Poverty Debate in Canada, 1970–1995

*Wendy McKeen*

UNIVERSITY OF TORONTO PRESS
Toronto Buffalo London

© University of Toronto Press Incorporated 2004
Toronto Buffalo London
Printed in Canada

ISBN 0-8020-8544-X

Printed on acid-free paper

**National Library of Canada Cataloguing in Publication**

McKeen, Wendy, 1954–
   Money in their own name : the feminist voice in poverty debate in
Canada, 1970–1995 / Wendy McKeen.

(Studies in comparative political economy and public policy)
Includes bibliographical references and index.
ISBN 0-8020-8544-X

1. Women – Government policy – Canada.   2. Canada – Social policy.
3. Poverty – Canada.   4. Feminism – Canada.   5. Women – Canada –
Social conditions.   6. Women – Canada – Economic conditions.
I. Title.   II. Series.
HQ1236.5.C2M325 2003      362.83′0971      C2003-902487-3

This book has been published with the help of a grant from the Canadian
Federation for the Humanities and Social Sciences, through the Aid to
Scholarly Publications Programme, using funds provided by the Social
Sciences and Humanities Research Council of Canada.

University of Toronto Press acknowledges the financial assistance to its
publishing program of the Canada Council for the Arts and the Ontario
Arts Council.

University of Toronto Press acknowledges the financial support for its
publishing activities of the Government of Canada through the Book
Publishing Industry Development Program (BPIDP).

# Contents

vi   Contents

# Preface

Canadian social policy is deeply biased in a way that detrimentally affects women, especially vulnerable groups of women, in their day-to-day lives, and this policy is working against any possibility for real gender equality. The problem is not explicit discrimination, as was previously the case, but that governments continue to ignore the issue of social reproduction and the bulk of unpaid care work carried out primarily by women. As feminists have argued, there is a major disjuncture between the economic system and the social policy system: we have a dual-breadwinner economic system harnessed to a single-breadwinner social policy system, and it is disproportionately women who are paying the price in terms of higher rates of poverty and growing stress levels. Under neo-liberalism, moreover, the social policy system has moved even further from recognizing social reproduction and the contribution of unpaid work to our society. Official policy has backed away from the blanket assumption that all women are dependents (i.e., are mothers and housewives) to adopt the equally damaging view that social context and social difference does not matter at all. Thus, single mothers on social assistance are being exhorted to enter the workforce, with little acknowledgment of, or real help with, their home and child care responsibilities. Social policy is also being refamilialized in many areas: for example, entitlement to child benefits and some aspects of Employment Insurance benefits are now based on total *household* as opposed to individual income. As feminists have identified, such criteria disproportionately disqualify women from benefits and reinforce the long-term cycle of their poverty (e.g., see Phipps et al., 2001). All of this has occurred as governments have abandoned a universalistic approach and embraced a more targeted and punitive one that places increasing amounts of responsibility on individuals and families for defending themselves against poverty and other social risks. Women's prospects for equality, then, continue to decline as growing numbers of them face the desperation of a life of juggling low-wage, contingent paid work with a growing burden of unpaid care and domestic work at home.

This book contributes to a recognition that these developments were not accidental – that they were, in fact, the result of complex and subtle processes that occurred largely between the mid-1970s and mid-1990s, in which both neo-liberal ideas prevailed, and radical, women-friendly alternatives were successfully resisted. I argue in this book that the second-wave women's movement *did* advance an alternative vision for social policy in the mid-1970s that was sophisticated and went right to the heart of the matter: the failure of state policy to recognize the social context of individual lives. The campaign ultimately failed to flourish, however, and this book is mainly concerned with understanding its defeat. While macro-level influences such as social and economic changes and the rise of neo-liberalism were critical, I highlight the constraining effects that the 'social policy community' had in shaping 'women's interests' in the field of federal social policy.

This book is important for two reasons. First, the alternative 'social individual' model for social policy that feminists advanced was a significant and far-reaching vision for change – one that still needs to be pursued if we are to solve issues of gender and other forms of inequality and work towards a more humane, solidaristic model for society. Second, this story has important lessons for understanding the politics of social policy in Canada more generally. Indeed, this book provides a concrete illustration of a position that is increasingly advanced within political studies – that the strategies and orientations of even marginalized political actors also count in shaping political debate and moving the agenda forward in particular directions. One of the findings of this study is that a wide range of organizations and social forces (most notably, left-liberal social policy and anti-poverty organizations) participated in shaping the parameters of the social reform process in ways that were readily incorporated into the emergent neo-liberal social policy regime, with its emphasis on targeting and its reassertion of a male-centred, familialist approach. In this new neo-liberal social policy landscape, gender issues and women's concerns have slipped from view, while in their stead stand 'Canadian children,' somehow stripped of their family connections and the gender relations they embody.

MONEY IN THEIR OWN NAME

# Introduction

The second-wave women's movement emerged in Canada over three decades ago with a new, and potentially radical, vision for Canadian social policy. While participants in this movement recognized and valued the many positive aspects of the Canadian social policy system, especially as it compared with what existed in the United States, they strongly opposed the way it entrenched notions of women's dependency. Like most social policy systems in the advanced welfare states, Canadian policy tended to treat women as mere appendages to their husbands insofar as their entitlement to benefits was based primarily on their status as a wife or mother (Eichler, 1983a; 1997; Haddad, 1986; Kitchen, 1980; 1986). Even benefits that were accessible to women as payment in their own name (e.g., the Family Allowance) were granted to them on the basis of their status as mothers. Feminists viewed this entrenched familialism as a major barrier to women's independence – women were disproportionately denied access to benefits under programs that tested for total family income – and they embarked on a campaign to shift the basis of entitlement from the family unit to the individual, so that women would be entitled to benefits in their own right. This would indeed appear to be a somewhat limited strategy for achieving equality for women from a contemporary feminist standpoint. As feminist analysts have pointed out, individualized entitlement on its own does nothing to address the gendered division of labour in which women are disproportionately assigned to child raising and domestic work, and only further penalizes those who do this work. This is especially evident in the current neo-liberal period in which the dominant approach within social assistance policy, for example, is to pressure lone mothers to enter paid work with little or no provision for their existing caring responsibilities. Yet, for feminists positioned in Canada in the early 1970s – a time and place wherein notions of social rights and social citizenship were fairly well accepted – this campaign was equally concerned with enhancing the visibility of married women and helping to expose the *social* significance of the unpaid care and domestic work they performed at home. It was, indeed, an attempt to establish a new model for social policy – one that recognized both the right to independence and the social and public relevance of unpaid domestic work.

In this book I ask why these efforts by feminists were not more successful in counteracting the dominant familialist and liberal-individualist constructions underpinning social policy, and why, indeed, feminists ultimately abandoned this course. My focus is limited to the activities of national women's organizations mainly outside of Quebec: the Quebec women's movement existed in a substantially different ideological and institutional environment and therefore constitutes a separate case. Moreover, while this sector of the women's movement struggled for individual entitlement in several policy areas that crossed all political scales – federal, provincial, and municipal – my focus is on the federal level debate on child and family benefits, that is, ranging from guaranteed annual income (or negative income tax) plans to child tax exemptions and credits, and the Family Allowance. The choice of policy area is partly a way of narrowing the topic, but this focus is an important one because these programs profoundly affect the daily lives of women and their families, providing both a critical source of independent income for women and buffering them against poverty. As John Myles and Paul Pierson (1997) have noted, moreover, negative income tax and guaranteed annual income policy (like the national child benefit program) is a key terrain on which the *new* politics of the welfare state are being played out and have defined key features of the neo-liberal welfare state. Thus, the study's focus, which spans a period of tremendous importance in welfare state change, from the heyday of social liberalism in the 1960s through to the neo-liberal restructuring that marked the mid-1990s, also provides an important window into understanding broader aspects of welfare state change in Canada.

The research process adopted for this study was one of triangulation among the theoretical-methodological framework, document analysis, and interviews with key informants. My analytic framework established the parameters and direction of my empirical research agenda and was revised in the process. My key source of data was published articles, reports, briefs, and submissions to legislative committees and commissions, produced by federal state actors, social policy and anti-poverty organizations, and organizations comprising the 'institutional-ized' women's movement. I used archival material to document the emergence in the 1960s of the poverty concept and feminist concerns with respect to women, social security, and poverty. I conducted in-depth interviews with key informants – individuals chosen mostly because of their involvement in social welfare and feminist politics in the period covered in this study (see Appendix). Finally, I used second-ary materials to substantiate my theories and supplement the empirical data.

My findings are that in the field of child and family benefits, femi-nists slowly but surely lost interest in their campaign for individualized benefits. What is important, however, is that there was clearly a gap between what feminists *might* have pushed for given their understand-ing of the issues and what they ended up supporting, namely, the shift to greater targeting. In explaining this discrepancy, I examine the inter-play of both *macro*-level and *meso*-level factors. Many macro-level fac-tors influenced feminist thinking and limited their choices, to be sure. They included, for example, the strength of liberalism (as opposed to socialism) as the dominant strain within the institutionalized women's movement, the growing preference of state and business interests for targeting measures, and the considerable erosion of feminist capacity to participate in social policy debate especially following deep cuts to their funding in the 1990s. My main focus goes beyond these issues, however, to examine how the nature of the decision context within which feminists were operating affected how they formed their ideals. I ask how did the universe of political discourse within the social policy community affect feminists' discursive space, their room to manoeu-vre? I argue that changes in the discourse on poverty generated largely by national social policy organizations – organizations with status as the 'progressive' voice on social policy – had a major influence in pushing feminists to reformulate their goals and demands to reflect more mainstream concerns.

At a minimum this book presents a corrective to the all too prevalent class-centred perspective on Canadian social policy development. Ig-noring the women's movement as an actor in this policy arena leaves out a vital part of the story. As Ann Porter (2003) has suggested, struggles by feminists and other groups to have the 'family' recognized, along-side the 'state' and 'market,' as a critical partner in provision of social welfare and to have the work and needs of caregivers recognized as a legitimate social policy concern, have indeed been a major force for change in the Canadian welfare state, particularly since the Second World War.

More centrally, this book presents a challenge to the theoretical perspectives often employed in contemporary studies of social policy, restructuring of the welfare state, and the politics of the women's movement, and it demonstrates the need within these scholarly areas to expand the scope of what is considered 'politics.' First, it argues for an approach that recognizes the importance of struggle over meaning or discourse, something that is often missing within mainstream political science accounts of politics, particularly the politics of social policy. Second, it insists on the importance of struggles within particular 'policy communities,' wherein narrower networks of political actors attempt to shape the debate in a specific policy area. The policy community perspective is especially important for exploring the ways the activities and discourses of politically *marginalized* organizations and social groups can make a difference in shaping politics and influencing the direction of policy change. As such, it is an important missing piece in many feminist accounts of politics, which are often limited to analysing the broader political terrain.

Too often analysis of welfare state politics has been attributed to 'neoliberalism' or the faceless force of globalization (Jessop, 1993). While these perspectives are indeed valuable, there is a growing sense that there are other, more complex, dynamic, and subtle aspects that need to be understood, as well. For example, political theorists are increasingly recognizing that political change, or indeed, regime shift, is not a simple top-down imposition by powerful actors, but the result of ongoing struggle and contestation by multiple actors whose discourses intermingle and mutually influence each other, albeit in ways that mostly favour the dominant view (e.g., Yeatman, 1990; Pringle and Watson, 1992; Larner, 2000; Dobrowolsky and Saint-Martin, 2002; Mahon, 2002). There is also mounting criticism, in this regard, of the influential 'pathdependency' approach to welfare state analysis (e.g., the work of Pierson, 1996; Myles and Pierson, 1997; Esping-Andersen, 1996, 1999) which posits that welfare states tend to change in ways that follow a predetermined path in accordance with the original (liberal, social-democratic, or conservative) welfare state model. Critics argue that this approach fails to focus sufficiently on the *dynamics* of politics, that it considers only a fairly narrow range of political actors, and/or does not take full account of the *creativity* of actors in posing challenges, offering solutions, and, thus, moving issues onto policy agendas (Dobrowolsky and Saint-Martin, 2002; Mahon, 2002; McKeen and Porter, 2003). It is indeed increasingly accepted that a range of political organizations and actors, from powerful to marginal, participate in welfare state politics. Their positions interact and mutually influence each other, albeit in ways that mainly favour those with power. The current study is not interested in 'blaming' progressive actors for neo-liberal changes. Clearly, neo-liberal actors and their cost-cutting motivations are the driving force behind the changes. Rather, it is interested in discovering the instances in which progressive actors felt compelled to modify their discourses and stances in order to continue to have a voice, and thus, have unwittingly lent their support to the neo-liberal model. Indeed, this book argues that the strategic activities of a number of prominent non-governmental organizations (NGOs) and interest groups – notably, left-liberal social policy and anti-poverty organizations, and at times, feminist organizations – served to facilitate, albeit inadvertently, the emergent neo-liberal social policy regime, with its preference for *targeted* policy. Likewise, I show that one consequence of the *failure* of Canadian feminists to establish an alternative, non-sexist, non-familialized model for social policy was greater political space in the early and mid-1990s for neo-liberal actors to embark on a strategy of refamilializing key areas of social policy. These developments of the mid-1980s to mid-1990s in many ways set the pattern for the political interests and initiatives that have followed since, including the new emphasis on child-focused policy as future 'investments' (Jenson and Saint-Martin, 2002).

In Chapter 1, I explore the problem of women's dependency in the family, the role of states in perpetuating such gender relations, and the reasons the strategy of seeking individualization of social policy is potentially more radical and far-reaching than is often conceded within contemporary feminist thought. In Chapter 2, I draw on various theoretical and political traditions – namely, post-structuralist perspectives on discourse, neo-Marxist and new political economy ideas about agency, and the public policy concept of the policy community – to develop at a new framework for understanding interest-shaping processes among marginalized political actors. Chapter 3 examines the renewed focus in Canada on the issue of poverty in the late 1960s, a focus that was critical for setting the terms and parameters for national debate about social policy. It also traces the emergence of the feminist voice on social policy and tensions that marked early feminist thinking on women and social policy. Chapters 4 to 6 focus on pivotal moments in social policy debate. These moments were selected not because they correspond to other major periodization criteria, such as shifts in political regimes or philosophies (although these shifts figure in the story), but because they were periods in which key debates on family benefits took place and in which feminists took critical stands. Chapter 4 examines the discursive turn in poverty discourse towards the 'feminization of poverty' and its effects in 'shaping' feminist approaches to child benefits during the debates in the mid- and late 1970s. Chapter 5 documents the moderate outlook of the left-liberal social policy sector and the constraints this placed on feminism during the early to mid-1980s term of the government of Prime Minister Brian Mulroney. Chapter 6 investigates the discursive and strategic turn to the issue of child poverty in the 1990s and, again, focuses on the ideological closures it presented for feminists. The concluding chapter presents a summary of my findings and claims and reflects on their implications for understanding broader aspects of change in the welfare state in Canada and contemporary shifts in policy, particularly as they affect women.

# CHAPTER ONE

# Solutions for Women-Friendly Social Policy: The Radical Potential of Individualized Entitlement

What should a woman-friendly, egalitarian form of citizenship and social policy look like, and what political demands will help to propel us towards such a vision? Feminist theorists of the welfare state have been engaged in this discussion for some time and have produced some important concepts. A key one, I believe, is that of the 'social individual,' or the idea that as individuals we all have social needs and responsibilities and that our ability to give or receive these are interdependent and intertwined (Winkler, 1998). The insights this presents allow us to critically assess the various kinds of demands feminists have traditionally made in the area of income support policy – most notably, the demand for more money for single mothers versus the demand for individualized entitlement. In this chapter I argue that the latter strategy of individualized entitlement has a radical potential for moving us towards a social individual model – a potential that has not generally been acknowledged within contemporary Canadian feminist thought. The starting point for my analysis, however, is the issue of women's dependency and how states are involved in perpetuating the problem.

## The Problem with Dependency

Feminists have long understood the profound debilitating effects that built-in assumptions of women's economic dependency have had on women and, indeed, society in general. As Ruth Lister (1995) has argued, the issue of dependency is problematic from the perspectives of philosophy, poverty, and power. The philosophical perspective argues that human freedom or autonomy is a basic human need and, as such, constitutes rights against the state: 'citizenship rights can be thought of as a measure of the autonomy an individual citizen enjoys as a result of his or her ... member[ship] of a society' (1995: 27). The implication is that governments have an obligation to bring into being or preserve the conditions whereby people can achieve autonomy. As Virginia Sapiro has pointed out, 'this is precisely what has been missing in a social policy which is content to prescribe dependency for women' (1990: 51). The argument has also been made within feminist jurisprudence that, with a view to justice, freedom, and dignity, individuals require a minimum amount of money for themselves and that economic dependency is the negation of freedom (Dahl, 1987: 111). Research substantiates that women experience the lack of personal income as a lack of dignity. From the perspective of poverty, both the ideology and actuality of women's economic dependency make women more vulnerable than men to poverty. As Jane Millar and Caroline Glendinning argue, 'women's financial dependency as reflected in welfare state legislation both legitimates and creates women's poverty ... Women's assumed dependence legitimates low pay and benefit systems which are indirectly discriminatory; their actual dependence contributes to material inequality and poverty within the home' (1987: 25, 26).

While Black feminists have pointed out that dependency is much less common among Afro-American and Afro-Caribbean women, who have historically been forced into the labour force as low-wage workers and to raise their families independently (Bhavnani and Coulson, 1986), the continued force of the ideology of women's dependency can still disadvantage a woman who is not actually dependent on a man (Lister, 1995: 26, 34). Indeed, social programs subject all women to the same imposition of familialism, based on a white, western notion of the family. Moreover, all but the most privileged women are governed by a wage and opportunity structure that favours male workers by constructing men as breadwinners and women only as secondary paid workers.

The effects of these ideologies and structures stretch far into the future, contributing to women's poverty in old age. The failure to recognize the family as a sphere of distribution has meant that historically women's poverty has only become visible upon family breakdown. Feminists have also highlighted how the distribution of resources within the family (including work, time, and money) is partly a function of power relationships, which in turn, reflect the independent economic contributions of each partner (Pahl, 1989; Lister, 1995). According to Barbara Hobson, power and dependency in the family operate as a two-way mirror: 'a woman's position in the market economy affects her bargaining position in the household; and a woman's position in the household (how unwaged work is divided) affects her earnings and potential earnings in the labor market' (1990: 238). The unequal power relationship that comes with full or partial economic dependency is experienced by women as a lack of control over resources, a lack of rights and a sense of obligation (contributing to 'compulsory altruism'), and deference (Lister, 1990: 451; 1995: 29; Pahl, 1989).

The effects on women can also be seen in women's lesser access to civil, political, and social rights of citizenship (Pascall, 1993). With respect to civil rights, while women have made substantial gains in legal rights, they are denied such rights in practice through violence and marital rape, and the lack of public intervention in this area. Another aspect of civil rights is the pressure on women to undertake caring work in the family. As Gillian Pascall has asked: 'to what extent do relationships of dependency within marriage and cohabitation allow women the freedom not to do unpaid work?' (1993: 117). Women's relatively lower incomes and security from paid work still make women dependent on the men with whom they live, and 'wifely duties ... are alive and well in practice' (ibid.). Women tend to feel an obligation to take on care work possibly because of a strong affection, but also often because of their subordinate positions in the labour market and the lack of alternatives. Moreover, taking up care labour often leaves women isolated and deprived of autonomy. With respect to political rights, women's commitment to their families and care work has been a major factor in their lack of representation in legislation and a barrier to their participation in political activities generally. Poor women are able to participate in political activities even less than poor men because of caring responsibilities (Nelson, 1984). In the area of social rights (rights derived from the market and social welfare policy), women's rights are undermined by systems of social provision that treat them as dependents. When many systems of social provision were established, the focus was on insuring breadwinners against disruptions in their earning, and no priority was given to attaching benefits to women's unpaid work. Today women's responsibility for care work limits their participation in paid work and their access to employment-linked social benefits. Although some benefits have been established to provide for parenthood or unpaid care, these are of lesser value than benefits for paid workers, and they are not at a level to allow financial independence. In most systems women make claims on the basis of their needs as mothers (e.g., social assistance, child benefits) or through derived entitlements as wives of paid workers (e.g., survivor benefits), while their needs as individuals go unrecognized. Women's claims to benefits are also often undercut by family-based means testing (MacDonald, 1998). Although the practice of employing the family as the unit of assessment is officially gender-neutral, the fact that men or husbands typically have higher incomes means that in practice women tend to be disentitled to benefits (Millar, 1989). Under the cohabitation rule – a rule that is commonly applied under needs-based social assistance programs – just the assumption that a live-in man is providing financial support is enough to disentitle a woman to benefits.

The questions that remain and continue to plague feminists are what are the alternatives and how can we get there? The question of whether there can be women-friendly social policy regimes has been a central one for feminist welfare state theorists of late. While there are perhaps no definitive answers, certain core principles have been identified.

### Seeking Solutions: Debates on Women-Friendly Policy

A critical point established by feminist social and political theorists is that the policies and practices of states are intimately involved in structuring gender relations and advancing or impeding women's access to full citizenship and autonomy. Earlier approaches to theorizing these issues were embedded in a functionalist and Marxist–feminist paradigm which viewed the welfare state as functioning on behalf of capitalism to ensure that women performed their role as unpaid domestic and care workers within the family (McIntosh, 1978; Wilson, 1977; Bryson, 1983; Land 1979). A body of historical and comparative analysis emerged – work that viewed these questions as historical and political, with a focus on political struggle in accounting for variation over time and across welfare state formations (e.g., Jenson, 1986; Hobson, 1990; Ruggie, 1984; Shaver, 1989; Nelson, 1990; Quadagno, 1990), and in which the state is viewed as a site of struggle rather than a coherent entity (Pringle and Watson, 1990). This new body of analysis allowed the possibility of women-friendly regimes to emerge and become a central focus. Indeed, a central question for discussion within contemporary feminist theory is how to conceptualize and achieve women-friendly welfare states. While the answers are not straightforward, there is I think agreement on some core concepts and principles. One of the major theoretical stumbling blocks in this endeavour has, of course, been the standard 'difference versus equality' debate within feminism. The questions it raises are whether to value care work or not, whether care work can provide the basis for citizenship for women, and whether it is possible for women to seek citizenship on the same footing as men. Posed concisely by Sylvia Walby, the question is: 'should women seek support for their existing roles in the family as carers, or should they be seeking to leave such roles behind and enter paid employment?' (1994: 387).

On the one hand, policies that ignore inequality of condition disadvantage women; and on the other, policies that encourage women alone to do caring work (e.g., payment for care work) further entrench the sexual division of labour. More recent theorizing has gravitated towards challenging the dichotomy. Constructing these options as opposite, or as incompatible, hides the fact that the standard underlying both sides is men as abstract individuals devoid of family commitments. The solution lies in challenging terms such as 'dependence' and 'independence' as ideological constructs: the independence that comes from working in the marketplace (men's independence) is often based on the hidden care and servicing work of others in the home (women's dependence). In other words, women's dependence facilitates the independence of others as workers and citizens (Lister, 1995). In reality, we are all interdependent. The real task, according to contemporary feminist analysts, is to establish a concept and vision of citizenship that recognizes the importance of care in society but does not lock women further into this role (Hirschmann and Liebert, 2001). In other words, the equality versus difference dilemma can be sidestepped by shifting the focus from women to men and to wider societal responsibility for care (e.g., Fraser, 1994; Lister, 1995). Part of the answer 'lies in problematizing men's failure to fulfil the obligations of citizen the carer' (Lister, 1995: 33) and 'to develop policies that discourage free riding ... the real free riders ... [are] men who shirk care work and domestic labour, and especially corporations who free ride on the labor of working people' (Fraser, 1994: 613).

Attending to, and to some extent cutting across, this 'care' debate, there is some agreement within the comparative feminist welfare state and citizenship literatures on at least two other core principles of women-friendly policy – principles that speak directly to the issue of women's responsibility for care work and the resulting dependency (i.e., a part that is missing in mainstream welfare state theory). The first is that access to paid work is important. Paid work has a particular relevance for women as a key route to financial independence or freedom from personal dependency. It has thus been a concern for women (especially married women) historically because of the official assumption in social programs and within male-dominated labour movements of the family model of the male breadwinner and dependent wife. The second principle, which has been advanced forcefully within recent feminist analyses of the welfare state, is that personal autonomy and independence for women (with caring responsibilities) is important, and this should be promoted through state policies (Orloff, 1993, 1997; O'Connor, 1993; Lewis, 1992, 1997; Ostner and Lewis, 1995; Sainsbury, 1994, 1996; Hobson, 1994; Jenson, 1997). This discussion emerged from the feminist critique of the notion of 'decommodification' defined as the degree to which individuals, or 'families,' can maintain an acceptable standard of living without reliance on market participation (Esping-Andersen, 1990; Korpi, 1989). Feminist theorists have argued that this formulation does not account for gender differences and needs to be complemented with a notion of autonomy – or, the degree to which individual adults can uphold a socially acceptable standard of living *independently of family relationships*, either through paid work or through social security provisions.[1] For Ann Orloff, a necessary measure of women's well-being is the extent to which states, through social provision and employment regulation, affect the capacity of individuals to form and maintain an *autonomous* household – to ensure the freedom from compulsion to enter a marital or other relationship (Orloff, 1993, 1997). Julia O'Connor has drawn out a similar construct in the notion that women's well-being depends on the extent to which states provide 'insulation from personal dependency,' which she views as being as important for women as 'insulation from public dependency.' She argues that 'the level of personal autonomy varies according to the range of services which insulate individuals from involuntary economic dependence on family members and/or involuntary dependence on state agencies' (O'Connor, 1993: 511, 512).[2]

Feminist scholars studying the issue of paying for care work have spoken of the need for a theoretical construct that is 'directly about men and women's relations to the family, rather than the market via the family' (McLaughlin and Glendinning, 1994: 64–5). They have advanced the theme of 'defamilisation' as a way of focusing not strictly on 'women's dependency on men,' but on the terms and conditions under which people engage in families and caring relationships: 'If decommodification is the process which varies the extent to which well-being is dependent on "our" relation to the cash nexus (Esping-Andersen, 1990: 35), then defamilisation is constituted by those provisions and practices which vary the extent to which well-being is dependent on "our" relation to the (patriarchal) family' (McLaughlin and Glendinning, 1994: 65).[3] These ideas are also embedded in Jane Lewis's proposition (1992; 1997) that the key to women's full citizenship is the enhancement of women's *choice* and that this ought to be the direction of social policy reform for women.[4]

While these are important formulations, they nevertheless fall somewhat short of a fully developed positive vision for a women-friendly regime. Indeed, a more far-reaching and integrated approach to defining women-friendly policy has been put forward by Celia Winkler (1998), and similar ideas have since been voiced by others (e.g., see articles in Hirschmann and Liebert, 2001). Winkler's claim is that in a democratic society people *do* have some things in common: all people share a need for care at various life stages (e.g., no one is ever just a 'mother,' everyone was also once a child), a need for material resources (e.g., pay), and a need to have a voice in society. An egalitarian policy regime will take account of these universals and recognize that they are interrelated and inextricably intertwined: the need for care, or to give care, affects one's ability to earn pay, and both affect on one's ability to participate politically. This formulation also suggests the importance of notions of social solidarity and community and a sense of belonging. Winkler arrived at this understanding through her analysis of the struggle of the feminist movement in Sweden for social policy in the late 1960s and early 1970s – a struggle that, as Winkler (1998) has described, was relatively successful in avoiding the pitfalls of the equality and difference opposition, in contrast to their U.S. counterparts in the contemporary period of welfare restructuring. Swedish demands for a universal child care system and a universal six-hour day reflected an approach to equality based on the perception of the model citizen as a 'social individual' and of society as composed of individuals who are both interdependent and contributing to society's well-being: 'Women were to be economically and politically independent from individual men, but in order for that to happen, the interdependence among care, material resources, and voice had to be acknowledged in concrete social arrangements' (Winkler, 1998: 155). That care, material resources, and voice are interwoven is demonstrated most vividly in the case of lone mothers, and it was *their* needs that became the standard on which Swedish feminists based their demands.

Moving from theory to practice presents further challenges, however. The question that needs to be asked is which strategies will best push state policy in ways compatible with the principle of defamilization and concept of 'social individualism'?

## From Theory to Political Demands: The Radical Potential of Individualization

A first and obvious point implied in the above discussion is that it is important to advocate for state policies that ensure women have access to good quality paid work, including the services that make employment a viable option. This has, in fact, been the primary focus of second-wave feminism (Lister, 1990; Orloff, 1993; O'Connor, 1996). Second, however, given that most women do not earn enough income through paid labour (because of part-time labour or care work), and that husbands do not always share their income, the traditional areas of *social* policy, most notably, income support programs, are an important site of struggle for women. The latter can be especially vital in giving women an independent income, albeit often minimal.

Looking more closely at the area of income support policy, two key strategies have been pursued historically, each falling on different sides of the equality or difference divide. On the 'difference' side – and in the current era, mostly associated with radical and liberal strands of feminism – there has been the attempt to obtain more generous and less stigmatizing social welfare benefits for single mothers. This has partly been an ideological struggle to construct single mothers as a 'deserving' category. On the 'equality' side, there has been a focus (mainly by white socialist-feminists within the contemporary period), on the eligibility criteria of social programs and the goal of shifting the basis of entitlement to benefits from the family unit to the individual. Family-based eligibility criteria (e.g., family-based tax systems and policies) impede women's participation in the labour force and affirm women's identity as secondary workers. Such criteria also tend to disqualify women from benefits on the grounds of the higher earnings of husbands. For example, comparative studies of family spending patterns indicate that many women in better-off social classes have their benefits clawed back under household calculation schemes, while women in less affluent households tend to see their benefits disappear into 'the household' (i.e., often meaning 'father's wallet'); (MacDonald, 1998; Phipps and Burton, 1996) ). These schemes, then, miss their mark when it comes to protecting the well-being of women and children and protecting them against poverty, as discussed earlier.

The important question is how do these strategies compare in their capacities to advance us towards the goals of defamilization and social individualism? Benefits for single mothers further women's capacity to establish an independent household, but they also exact a high price from women. Programs that provide benefits for single mothers have nearly always employed family-based eligibility criteria, and in the immediate term this has often meant that women are tied to individual, often abusive, men, and deprived of their autonomy (Mosher, 2000). Over the long term, such programs have reinforced familial ideology and with it the gendered division of labour through which women serve as unpaid providers of care, the notion of women's dependency within the family, and their identity as 'relations' (e.g., 'mothers') rather than 'individuals' (Sainsbury, 1996: 195–6). The significance of the latter has been underlined by Winkler in her critique of the 'care allowance' (payment for care). Drawing on Susan James's work, Winkler argues that it is only in seeing oneself as an *individual* as opposed to a *relationship* (such as mother) that one acquires the emotional independence that is a prerequisite for voice in a democratic society. Emotional independence requires an ability to transcend one's local and immediate needs to recognize the ways in which we are all, in fact, interdependent (Winkler, 1998: 162). Feminists have, indeed, consistently waged campaigns to attain individual rights within the context of these programs (e.g., challenges to the 'spouse in the house' rule), although progress continues to be limited.

The second course – individualization of entitlement – is in one sense an essential, but limited, strategy – *essential* as a long-term strategy for challenging the familialist, breadwinner and dependent ideology that underlies most social policy systems, but *limited* because as a 'sameness' approach to achieving equality for women it ignores inequality of conditions that disadvantage women in the first place. Misgivings towards individualized entitlement have tended to increase as an individualist philosophy is ever more advanced under a neo-liberal agenda. Under neo-liberalism, the fundamentals of social citizenship are being transformed into a profoundly *anti-social* form of individualism in which individuals are being held responsible for their own 'dependency,' structural inequalities are obscured, and the value of difference is denied altogether. In this scenario, women are cast as 'bad' citizens, and the women's movement is constructed as a ghetto of the disadvantaged ('losers'?; Brodie, 1996a). This perspective has been echoed by feminists examining the recent shifts in social assistance towards an individualized, gender-neutral approach. Under these systems, women are expected to perform like men as workers, but without the provision of support services such as day care and job training that allow them to overcome the structural barriers that disadvantage them in the labour market (e.g., Scott, 1996; Evans, 1996). Those who have researched the needs of dependent caregivers have insisted that while individualization is necessary, it needs to be complemented at a minimum by short-term strategies that support women who currently perform unpaid caring work with little or no financial or practical support (Lister, 1995: 23, 24; Finch, 1990: 52; Luckhaus, 1994: 161). Feminist analysts of social security likewise support the need for 'more nuanced alternatives to the lone individual versus the nuclear family as the unit for policy analysis' (MacDonald, 1998: 4).

While not disputing the above assessments, they do tend to overlook something of value in the demand for individualization that emerges especially when we reflect on Winkler's concept of the social individual. Pursuing individualization within a context of classical liberalism or neo-liberalism leads to the kinds of anti-women arrangements referred to earlier, to be sure. If individualized entitlement is being pursued, however, within a policy environment wherein established universalistic rights and ideals of social responsibility and human interdependence are already accepted, it serves well to promote the 'social' strain of individualism based on 'independence within interdependence,' and thus to a fundamental questioning of the status quo. Indeed, it provides an important avenue for bringing care work out of the private and into the public realm, giving care workers a voice in political debate, and establishing the necessary conditions for individuality and sense of community to flourish. These are all prerequisites for a truly egalitarian society.

## The Empirical Questions of this Book

It is this deeper sense of possibilities inherent in the struggle to individualize social policy that inspired the subject of this book, which is the historical path taken by Canadian feminists to achieve a women-friendly, defamilialized model in the realm of federal child benefits and, specifically, their successes and losses with respect to achieving individualized entitlement. This project is not as straightforward as it first appears, primarily because I accept that political interests are not given, as liberal-pluralists imagine, but are shaped rather as actors struggle 'on the ground' within specific historical circumstances – particular material, ideological, and discursive contexts. By the same token, we cannot assume that women and feminists are a homogeneous group that will always recognize their long-term interests or want to realize them. The basis of women's unity is never given but must be constructed, and it is threatened by differences of class, race, ethnicity, and nationality (Molyneux, 1985). 'Strategic gender interests' are not always going to be accepted by all women at all times (hence there are liberal, socialist, radical strains of feminism); the pursuit of strategic gender interests can threaten the short-term 'practical interests' of some women or result in a loss of protection that they cannot afford.[5] In this book, then, I interrogate and attempt to understand the *shaping* of the political interests of the women's movement within the terrain of federal child and family benefits from the early 1960s to the mid-1990s, with an eye to assessing the possibilities and limitations for bringing questions to do with women's autonomy to the fore. Before proceeding with this history, however, it is important to understand how the political interests of new or marginalized political actors are formed, and this is the topic of the next chapter.

# CHAPTER TWO

# Understanding How the Interests of New Political Actors Are Shaped: Discourse, Agency, and 'Policy Community'

> Men make their own history, but they do not make it as they please; they do not make it under self-selected circumstances, but under circumstances existing already, given and transmitted from the past.
>
> (Karl Marx, *The Eighteenth Brumaire of Louis Napoleon*, 1852, Chapter 1)

Post-structuralist, neo-Marxist theorists declare that political identities and interests are shaped by actors in the course of political struggle within historically specific material, institutional, and ideological and/ or discursive contexts which structure their political opportunities and closures. Starting with this position, this chapter asks what factors, forces, and/or processes matter most in shaping the political interests of a *new* or *emerging* political identity? Important insights into this question are found, for example, in contemporary feminist analyses of the strength of the feminist movement in Canada. Suzanne Findlay's work offers one approach. She argues that women's concerns are transformed and depoliticized as the outcome of the process of institutionalization within state discourse.[1] Findlay presents the case of the struggle for employment and pay equity in Ontario in the 1980s and 1990s. While feminists started out with radical demands that were inclusive of all women workers, the issues and definitions of the problem were gradually narrowed, as feminists were compelled to make compromises with the officials and bureaucracies of the state and other dominant interest groups (e.g., unions). The legislative approach finally adopted (but now defunct) was inadequate in that it was based on a model for pay equity that ignored the low wages of women working in community organizations and other exclusively female workplaces.

A second approach to understanding feminist politics is typlified in the theme 'the state organizes women's interests.' This current has emphasized the power of macro (neo-liberal) state discourses and practices in legitimizing, or delegitimizing, interest groups and their claims.[2] For example, Janine Brodie (1995) has argued that neo-liberalism's individualizing ideology, in which the poor and marginalized are blamed for their situations, and structural inequalities and disadvantages are ignored, has served to delegitimize social movements that challenge inequality, especially the women's movement.

While these are important perspectives on interest-shaping processes, I argue that a more complete perspective can be acheived by understanding the significance of struggle within the 'policy community.' Political agency takes shape as actors make choices in relation to particular *policy* issues and debates and under the influence of both macro-level, but also, policy community-level, factors. Below I examine three core concepts in political theory – namely, discourse, agency, and the 'policy community' – which I maintain combine to give us a promising new framework for exploring the processes of interest-shaping among marginalized political actors.

## Discourse

A central claim of post-structuralist theory is that language and discourse are important in shaping politics and political interests, based on a more fundamental claim that social reality is not fixed and has no intrinsic meaning. As Rosemary Pringle and Sophie Watson describe, 'there has been an emphasis on the relational, historical, and precarious character of "reality"' (1992: 64). Identities and subjectivity are produced in discursive practices, the meanings of which are a site of constant struggle and conflict (ibid.). Discourses shape ideas (ideology). They are problem-setting frameworks, or sets of statements that 'define, describe, and delimit what it is possible to say and not possible to say ... with respect to the area of concern ... A discourse ... organizes and gives structure to the manner in which a particular topic, object, process is to be talked about' (Kress, 1985: 6, 7).

This thinking has important implications for conceptualizing social problems. As Anna Yeatman suggests, for instance, state policy is not as a response to a social problem 'out there,' but *constitutes* the problem to which it is seeming to respond (1990: 158). Moreover, in constituting social problems, policies also constitute the claims on the political process and, therefore, the claimants making the claims. In constructing child abuse as a social problem, for example, the state also constitutes new 'claims' on the political process – by advocates on behalf of children, by parents, by those resisting the politicization of parenting, and potentially, by children (1990: 170).[3] The core labels chosen for a given policy are, thus, a critical *political* issue. Yeatman provides an example in the use of 'family' versus 'parents': policy in relation to families 'can be vaguely swathed in ritual and rhetoric,' while policy for 'parents' has to be specific and concrete in providing assistance for people who parent (1990: 155). An illustration of this point in the Canadian social policy context can be seen in the approach adopted by the Mulroney government in the late 1980s under the rubric of addressing 'child poverty.' The policies announced focused on developmental issues related to *children*. These initiatives, announced in 1992, focused on health development during pre- and post-natal periods, infancy, and early childhood (Canada, Health and Welfare Canada, 1992), as opposed to the real problem of the high unemployment and low wages of the children's *parents*.[4]

A critical point established by this perspective, then, is that the struggle over meaning is an essential part of politics, or put differently, that politics always entails the struggle over meaning, with discourse itself constituting 'the power which is to be seized' (Yeatman, 1990: 155). As Yeatman puts it: 'If politics involves the reduction of complexity by means of decisions and policies, the field of political activity comprises all those who seek to affect and to contest how the agenda of policy-making gets framed. Political activity itself becomes preeminently a politics of contest over meaning: it comprises the disputes, debates and struggle about how the identities of the participants should be named and thereby constituted, how their needs should be named and thereby constituted, how their relationships should be named and thereby constituted' (ibid.).

## Agency

The second core idea, articulated especially within neo-Marxist and new social movement theory, is the importance of agency (within a structural context) for understanding politics and social change. This perspective rejects the totalizing view of discourse in which texts are given all of the power and no allowance is made for the creativity and power of human beings (Jenson, 1990: 66). It recognizes that people, not discourses, create meaning and reality – subjectivity, identity, interests – through their creative actions and that it is only in recognizing the possibility of *agency* that we can account for opposition and contestation (Jenson, 1990: 66). This body of work emphasizes the creativity of actors in 'naming' themselves and others, and in 'framing' their issues, thereby *mobilizing* interests and *making* their opportunities. A name, for instance, allows a collective actor to represent itself to itself and to outsiders. The choice of a name affects a collectivity's strategies for making claims on the political system by helping to generate strategic resources, setting discursive boundaries such that some claims become more meaningful and others less so, and locating the movement in relation to others and, therefore, presenting possibilities for alliances and identifying opponents. The choice of a name also has consequences for how claims are routed through state institutions (Jenson, 1995: 116). Through the activity of framing, actors are giving meaning to an object, situation, event, or experience, and in this way are constructing claims about the nature of the problems, causes, solutions, and rationales for joining a cause – with respect to their own cause as well as the causes of other relevant sets of actors (Snow and Benford, 1992: 137; Hunt et al., 1994: 203). For example, as Jenson has pointed out, the post-1960s innovation of the name 'Québécois' (as opposed to French Canadians) to describe French-speaking citizens of Quebec made it possible for Quebec provincial governments and nationalists to put forward a claim that Quebec was a distinct *nation* as opposed to a distinct *language group*. Likewise, the new name and identity 'women,' which was adopted in the 1960s by the second-wave women's movement to describe female persons, made possible a new claim that all women were different from all men and that as a group women suffered from discrimination. It was also critical for generating a sense of solidarity among women, something that was not possible under the name 'ladies' (Jenson, 1994). As some of this work recognizes, however, 'not all identities, names, frames, or advocacy strategies are possible' (Phillips, 1994b: 196). Some actors and/or groups are not able to realize their identities, or are excluded. Whether a particular identity or set of interests will emerge, and what weight it will have, depends on the specific material conditions, dominant discourses, and particularly, the prevailing power relations, within which actors act.[5]

Jane Jenson (1995) has made an important contribution in developing and conveying this structure-and-agency balanced view of social and political change and stasis, with her concept of the 'universe of political discourse.' It is, indeed, an important tool for capturing the dual notion that political action is both shaped by, and can shape (alter), structural context – an unpacking of Karl Marx's famous formulation cited at the beginning of this chapter (Phillips, 1990: 66). The 'universe of political discourse' constitutes the universe of socially constructed meaning produced in the course of, and resulting from, political struggle. It is a terrain on which meaning systems jostle for attention and legitimacy as actors seek to name themselves to themselves and to others, and have their causes, positions, and demands respected and met (Phillips, 1994b). This terrain 'filters and delineates claims, and, in fact, determines what is "political" in the first place' by way of limiting the range of actors, issues, and policy alternatives considered legitimate and/or feasible and the alliance strategies available for achieving change (Phillips, 1996: 257). Prevailing social relations, usually reflecting the unequal balance of power in society, ensure that greater weight is given to some identities, interests, and claims, and not others, such that some will be privileged in public debate and others will simply be absent from it. Patricia Collins (1989) provides an interesting concrete example of this in her finding that the invisibility of the poverty of Black women in U.S. poverty studies is not because 'no problem exists' (as a pure constructivist would maintain), but because of the relatively little power of Black women in making claims, and the biases of white analysts themselves which prevent them from 'seeing' this problem. Institutions play a key role – prevailing social relations are materialized within, and reproduced over time by institutions, which also provide a terrain for action (Jenson 1995: 115). State institutions, for example, have enormous power in establishing the terms of inclusion and exclusion by recognizing some actors as legitimate. The availability of allies and the power of opponents also affect a group's opportunity for making claims. Susan Phillips uses the concept of the 'political opportunity structure' (developed in the work of both Jenson and Sydney Tarrow) to describe these constraints (1994b: 196). Influence over the universe of political discourse is jealously guarded so that collectivities attempting to introduce new actors, issues, and policy alternatives must overcome the resistance of what is already established (Jenson, 1987: 66). Since power is relational rather than unidimensional, however, there may be opportunities and spaces for resistance to, and contestation of, imposed definitions of identities and issues.[6] Thus, as Jenson emphasizes, while there are periods of stability in which both proponents of change and defenders of the status quo share a common language of politics, there can also be moments of instability, or crises, in which alternative voices may emerge to challenge and modify the hegemonic understandings (Jenson, 1993; Brodie et al., 1992: 7). Structures are thus created, recreated, and changed by actors in struggle (Jenson, 1995: 115).

The key points we can take from the approach described here are that political agency is shaped as actors (through their choices and policy stances) attempt to influence policy and discourse within historically specific material, institutional, and ideological and discursive environments; that macro-level variables, such as socioeconomic conditions, the priorities of the government in power, and the broad universe of political discourse, are all critical in shaping the political context; that socioeconomic conditions provide the 'raw materials' within which actors must work to develop their discursive interpretations; that political agendas and discourses of state actors and other powerful interests specify the broad parameters of debate, including the policy issues to be addressed and the options considered feasible; and that macro-political discourses and institutional arrangements also determine the demeanour of the state vis-à-vis the claims of social movements and therefore, affect the ability of any interest group or social movement to make new claims or alter dominant understandings.

Public policy theory has given us another key insight into politics, however, which is that much political struggle actually takes place as debates over particular *policies* (or a single policy). As I argue below, it is by combining the above insights with the notion of 'policy community' that we gain an important new, and more complete, approach to understanding political struggle and the factors that shape it.

## Policy Community

The idea that political struggle most often takes place as debates over policy is especially pertinent for understanding how the outlooks and demands of new or emerging political actors or movements are shaped. A useful point of departure for this focus is the mainstream field of structural-institutionalist public policy, whose strength has been its attention to the policy level. Studies in this area are broadly concerned with explaining policy outcomes in particular fields by examining structural factors at the meso-level – such as the internal organizational capacities and level of development of state versus societal actors and the structure or pattern of the relationships or linkages between them – that are seen as all more or less influenced by broader institutional macro-political variables (Coleman and Skogstad, 1990: 17).[7] One of the key claims of this work is that political struggle takes place around specific policy issues and involves a closed set of political actors. As Paul Pross (1986) has suggested, the entire political community is rarely involved in policy debate; the policy system relies on specializations – 'specialized publics' or 'policy communities' that, because of their 'functional responsibilities,' 'vested interests,' and 'specialized knowledge,' are allowed by society and the public authorities to dominate the decision-making and determine public policy in a specific field of activity (1986: 98). While there are gradations among them, members of the policy community are said to have shared, or commonly understood, belief systems, codes of conduct, and established patterns of behaviour. They also have varying degrees of power to define the terms of the debate, ranging from the inner core of policy-makers (termed, the 'sub-government') to groups and individuals who are interested in influencing certain policies but do not participate in policy-making (termed, the 'attentive public').[8]

The policy community concept as it stands has certain limitations that we should not ignore, however. It embeds liberal-pluralist assumptions (e.g., that groups compete to influence public policy on more or less equal terms), which make it less useful for grasping all aspects of political struggle. For example, while practitioners of this approach might acknowledge differences of power *within* the policy community (as in the distinction between the 'sub-government' and 'attentive public'), they do not generally acknowledge the *constructed* nature of political interests and the broader terrain of power relations within which political actors are embedded. This means that they are not generally able to make visible the political parameters of a policy debate or reveal potential challenges to the dominant paradigm or discourse. Rodney Haddow's work on the poverty policy community in Canada is one such example (1990; 1993). Haddow's study assumes *poverty* as an organizing theme, from which the 'poverty community' (consisting of organizations concerned with poverty) comes into being. Yet, his focus on progressive actors within the community is limited to the specific grouping of primarily liberal or left-liberal organizations that state officials are willing to recognize, while ignoring groups standing in the wings who represent more radical and/or oppositional discourses and perspectives (such as, e.g., Marxist, labour, and feminist groups). His work is, thus, not able to reveal the possible challenges posed by these marginalized interests to the *liberal* paradigm and to the concept of poverty itself.[9] In another sense, this approach generally fails to appreciate the importance of discourse and meaning construction to politics: only by problematizing meaning construction can we fully explain the continued resonance of 'poverty' as a public and political issue and begin to question when and where potentially competing ideologies exist, but are suppressed, marginalized, and fail to flourish.

The important point here is that this mainstream policy community concept can be recast as a more useful theoretical tool by setting it against and beside Jenson's broader perspective of the 'universe of political discourse.'[10] The latter approach shows the relevance, when thinking about policy communities, of the broad set of power relations prevailing in society, including the overall demeanour of the state towards oppositional interests or social movements. There may be times, for instance, when the state is relatively permeable vis-à-vis the voices of civil society, and more willing to nurture these groups, and other times when it is more insulated. It raises questions about the parameters and make-up of the policy community: policy communities are political constructs that change over time. For example, we can ask why only some interest groups or social movments (out of the full range of such groups) ever attain legitimacy and recognition as 'spokes-groups' on the issues, while others are marginalized and silenced. It also suggests the importance of viewing a policy community as being in some sense a microcosm 'universe of political discourse' with its own dominant discourses that condition political action – but keeping in mind that struggle on this plane is both influenced by, and influences, broader political developments and debates. It is important to ask, for example, in what ways dominant discourses within policy communities shape political action. This framework opens up the possibility that other established interest groups even within the relatively powerless 'attentive public' (as opposed to the powerful 'sub-government') can play a critical role in setting the terms and conditions for new actors participating in debates in the field and influencing the ways the latter groups define their goals in the area.

Coming back to my original question concerning the factors that matter most in shaping the politics of emerging political groups, combining these ideas suggests the following analytic framework: the political interests of newly emerged groups are formed as a result of their making choices, or taking policy stands, within the context of particular policy debates – debates that take place among a limited set of actors or organizations – ranging, for instance, from powerful state actors to marginal (oppositional) ones. The parameters of the debates and important aspects of the policy community (e.g., the line between 'insiders' and 'outsiders') are clearly defined by broad macro-level material, institutional, and ideological and discursive conditions (e.g., growing poverty, the mounting of a major policy review, the promotion of a new philosophy, such as targeting, and so on). Constraints and opportunities can also be generated, however, from within the policy community itself, and these can have a direct influence on the political options available to less powerful actors. It is reasonable to assume, for instance, that the discursive constructions (e.g., reflecting particular interpretations of the problems and their solutions) and political tactics of certain organizations – especially those that are in some sense natural, potential allies – are among the important factors conditioning the ideas of, and avenues available to, new contenders seeking a voice in the field.

This approach shares much ground with the perspectives on feminist politics outlined earlier, to be sure. For example, it has much in common with Suzanne Findlay's perspective on the institutionalization of women's issues, in which feminist ideals were seen as having been co-opted into a more general position that reflected the terms acceptable to other dominant actors. My own approach differs somewhat insofar as I am introducing the idea of another sphere of political activity – the 'policy community' and its universe of political discourse – that exists in interplay with the prevailing sociopolitical conditions, to condition and set limits on the goals of marginal social movements. Feminist choices concerning the definition of problems and issues in any policy area are thus influenced in the first place by the ideas and discursive constructions of more dominant groups within the policy community that are positioned as *allies*. While the second approach I discussed earlier – the thesis that 'the state organizes women's interests'– is valuable indeed, I am suggesting that there is more to the story: a macro-level focus is necessary, but not sufficient, for revealing the complex and subtle nature of the contemporary political struggle. Indeed, it is within the more intimate arena of the policy community that the choice-making activities of peripheral actors are more likely to come into view and we are able to ask questions about the significance and consequences of these choices – for instance, whether they serve to uphold and legitimize dominant understandings and the dominant paradigm or whether they challenge it. My argument is simply that these existing perspectives on politics need to be balanced out with interrogations that place weight on struggles within policy communities and the difference that the political and strategic choices of marginalized social forces can have in shaping politics and, indeed, new policy regimes.

The remainder of this book examines the history of feminist involvement in the federal terrain of family and child benefits policy. While it treats both macro- and meso-oriented factors as significant in shaping feminist choices, the primary focus is on the meso-terrain – primarily because this is an aspect that has been overlooked in studies that have attempted to understand feminist activity in Canadian public policy. Each of the next three chapters begins with a description of the macro-social, -economic, -political, and -discursive environment, taking into account socioeconomic conditions of the period (i.e., the state of the economy, employment, poverty, the family, and women's roles) and the broad political milieu and universe of political discourse. With respect to the latter, attention is paid to the tone of the relations between state and groups in civil society and the broad parameters of the national social policy debate, including the ideals for social policy advanced by both state and progressive or oppositional actors. They turn then to feminist politics, and I attempt to uncover and explain the political and strategic choices made by feminists, with the major focus on the policy stands they took in the realm of social policy and child benefits on the issue of autonomy and individualization of entitlement. The first of these chapters interrogates the origins of the modern social policy community and debate in Canada, especially the influence within social policy debate of the left-liberal sector and newly emerged feminist movement.

# CHAPTER THREE

# The Mainstream Poverty Debate in the 1960s and the Emergence of a Feminist Alternative

Two significant developments took place in the period of the 1960s to the early 1970s. First, the basic contours of the contemporary social policy community and social policy debate took shape in this period, as a range of actors came together under the rubric of addressing 'poverty.' Of particular interest is that established, nationally focused social policy and anti-poverty organizations, whose interests centred on poverty and redistribution, secured their place at this time as the 'progressive voice' in the debate. Second, was the emergence of a potentially important new participant in social policy debate, the institutionalized 'second-wave' women's movement. In this chapter I explore the nature and parameters of the new national social policy debate that took shape and examine the initial interests of the fledgling women's movement on issues of social policy, including the movement's perspective on the question of autonomy and individualized rights. I argue that among the various issues and critiques that feminists expressed was the kernel of a novel and potentially far-reaching vision for social policy reform based on social-democratic and radical feminist sensibilities.

The chapter begins with a discussion of the macro-level conditions that shaped the social policy environment in the period 1960 to 1974 or so. It then turns to examine the left-liberal (progressive) sector of the social policy community and the new-found voice of women.

## 'Social Liberalism' and New Parameters for a National Social Policy Community

A snapshot of the Canadian welfare state taken around 1960 would reveal it to be 'liberal' in character with some important 'social democratic' impulses (in keeping with the terms developed by Gøsta Esping-Andersen (1989)). Its liberalism lay in its 'residual' orientation or idea that state intervention should be minimal relative to the family and market – it should occur only after the family and the market fail. In typical liberal fashion, Canadian social policy was dominated by means-tested assistance programs run by the provinces and municipalities in which the benefits provided were miserly, meant to be short term, and often punitive and stigmatizing. The recipients were mainly highly visible persons (e.g., the blind, the disabled, or single mothers) who were classified as unemployable and therefore deserving of benefits (Haddow, 1993; Myles, 1996). Both during and after the Second World War, however, Canada's social policy system acquired important universalistic (citizenship-based) and insurance-based elements (its social-democratic components) evident in such developments as a national program of Unemployment Insurance (1940), the Family Allowance (1944), and Old Age Security (1951). Changes took place in the Canadian welfare state and universe of political discourse in the 1960s, however, which together marked a shift to what Rianne Mahon and others have called 'social liberalism' – a 'social democratic' as opposed to 'laissez-faire' liberalism (Mahon 1997a; 1997b; O'Connor et al., 1999; Jenson et al., 2003). Along with important changes to social programs the period ushered in new ideologies, discourses, and themes that set the parameters for a new national social policy debate, the legacy of which is with us today. Policy innovations and expansions were made feasible by the relative economic security of the early and mid-1960s with its growing economy, rising incomes, and relatively low rates of unemployment and inflation (Canada, Royal Commission on the Economic Union and Development Prospects for Canada, 1985; Brodie and Jenson, 1980; Rice, 1985). Their materialization, however, was due in part to pressure exerted by new social groups representing the marginalized (which in Canada included aboriginal peoples, youth, women, the poor, and ethnic, cultural, and language groups), the growing nationalist movements in Quebec and English Canada, the then-powerful labour unions, and the social-democratic New Democratic Party (Jenson and Phillips, 1996; Haddow, 1993; Mahon, 1997a). With the themes of national identity, equity, social justice for the marginalized, and democratic participation gaining a foothold in the ruling Liberal party, a number of new social programs were introduced which, as analysts have noted, made the social benefits available to Canadians even more distinct from those available in the United States (Jenson and Phillips, 1996: 116, 117; Myles, 1996: 136). They included, between 1965 and 1971, universal health insurance (in 1968), extended cost-sharing in health and education (the Established Programs Financing Act, 1964), major reform of social assistance (the Canada Assistance Plan, or CAP, in 1966), substantial improvements to unemployment insurance including the addition of sickness benefits (in 1971), and two new old age pension programs – the first national contributory pension plan (the Canada and Quebec Pension Plans, in 1966, and the Guaranteed Income Supplement in 1967 (Haddow, 1993; Myles, 1996; Ursel, 1992). These program changes also represented a substantial expansion of federal responsibility for meeting social need. The CAP, for instance, which provided for federal and provincial sharing of the cost for social assistance and social services, marked the first time the federal state took on responsibility for social services and income assistance for single mothers (the latter having been covered previously under provincial categorical assistance programs). The instrument of CAP illustrates another aspect of the social liberal shift – the incorporation of social-democratic notions of collectivism and citizenship rights into an otherwise liberal (selective and targeted) program. For instance, CAP provided for a range of social services to enable independence (e.g., day care, homemakers' services, health, counselling, rehabilitation, community development), required national standards, employed the more humane needs test as opposed to means test, and provided an appeal mechanism (Moscovitch, 1996; Little, 1999).

The social liberal character of policy reform was matched by the new openness of the federal state to the claims of emerging social movements and collective interests. Claims for access and claims on behalf of groups to redress past wrongs could be heard, although by no means did this constitute 'equal' access (Jenson and Phillips, 1996: 119). The themes of community development and citizen participation also became integral to Liberal governance. From the mid-1960s to the early 1970s, the Canadian federal state provided a significant amount of funding to the voluntary sector and various interest and advocacy groups, including (via the Department of Secretary of State, Citizenship Branch) multicultural groups, official language minorities, and the socially disadvantaged, especially women, aboriginal groups, youth, and social action groups such as those representing 'militant poor peoples' (Loney, 1977; Felt, 1978; Pal, 1993, Haddow, 1993; Jenson and Phillips, 1996).

Certain discourses and themes were more powerful than others, however, in capturing the public imagination and shaping debate on social reform, including a sense of who should be represented in the debate. 'Poverty' was one such master discourse. 'Poverty amidst affluence' was discovered in Canada as unemployment and inflation climbed in the mid- and late 1960s. Similar discoveries were made in several other western nations.[1] The emergence of poverty as a prominent public issue was also partly paved by the civil rights movement in the United States and the rise of social movements of the marginalized. Much of the discourse on poverty was, nevertheless, carefully orchestrated by the dominant federal Liberal Party and the governmental agencies and commissions struck to address the issue. The federal Liberals announced a 'war on poverty' in April 1965, following a like announcement by the U.S. president in 1964, and the federal state and quasi-governmental bodies led the way in the late 1960s in researching the issue and collecting data. A research and coordinating body, the Special Planning Secretariat, was established within the Office of the Privy Council, for example. The secretariat's reports, most notably the one entitled *Meeting Poverty – Profile of Poverty in Canada* (1965), were critical in initially defining the problem, as were other studies carried out for the Liberal Party, such as one prepared for the Harrison Liberal Conference held in Harrison Hot Springs, British Columbia, in November 1969 (e.g., Head, 1969). The Economic Council of Canada, or ECC (1968) and the Special Senate Committee on Poverty, chaired by Senator David Croll, which had been struck on the advice of the ECC (Canada, Parliament, 1971), were also important in drawing public attention to the issue and placing reform of social security onto the public agenda. Further support was provided by both academic and more popular texts such as W.E. Mann's book entitled *Poverty and Social Policy in Canada* (1970), John Harp and John Hofley's book *Poverty in Canada* (1971), and, further to the left, Ian Adams et al.'s publication *The Real Poverty Report* (1971), and Ian Adams,'s book *The Poverty Wall* (1970). An important focus of these works was *measuring* poverty. The key reference for this was the statistical report on poverty, entitled *Incomes of Canadians*, by Jenny Poloduk (1968) of the Department of Statistics. Podoluk followed the approach of Mollie Orshansky's statistical profiles of poverty in the United States prepared in the early 1960s.[2]

Poverty was not just a neutral, unbiased concept, however. It was given a particular meaning by the dominant actors at the time, and it structured political options and debates in social policy in particular ways. The concept of poverty injected some compassion and lightness into public discourse and played into a new vision of what it meant to be a Canadian, to be sure. Discussions of poverty were, indeed, often sites wherein links were forged between the themes of justice and equity and those of national identity, in keeping with the thesis advanced by Jane Jenson and Susan Phillips (1996). We see evidence of this, for example, in the following excerpt from a pamphlet on poverty published by the Office of the Privy Council (1967: 11–12):

If we draw a profile of a Canadian living in poverty, he looks like this:

- He lives in a substandard, crowded home;
- He has a poor education;
- His health is bad;
- His income is low;

And as for the stream of Canadian life – socially, economically, politically, culturally, he's not with it.

His living conditions are bad because his income is low. His education is poor, probably because he came from a poor home. His health is bad because his living conditions are bad and always have been bad. His income is low because he has poor health and a poor education.

And he, too, is a Canadian.

The poverty concept conveyed the more humanistic and social messages that were a part of social liberalism – the ideals of human dignity, decency, compassion, and justice. These were underscored by a connotation that poverty was the result of structural features of the economy and modern technological life rather than of individual personal failings. The poor were portrayed as innocent victims of larger structures that were beyond their control:

Widespread poverty exists in Canada in the midst of affluence, not because of individual inadequacy or original sin, but because of an economic system which utilizes technological invention to the maximum degree in its pursuit of increasing production and profits. (Head, 1969: 8)

The poor, after all, are not, as some still pretend, poor of their own accord. The poor have no uncommon moral flaw that sets them apart, let alone condemns them. They are casualties of the way we manage our economy and our society. (Canada, Parliament, Special Senate Committee on Poverty, 1971: xxvii)

This new level of humanism was also expressed in the view that poverty was a *relative* feeling of inequality and indecency created by comparison with the standards and lifestyles of others: 'in the affluent society, the poor man feels poorer' (Schlesinger, 1972: 6, 7).' This view contrasted distinctly with the *absolutist* definition of poverty that continued to dominate in U.S. discourse.

This humanistic and sympathetic approach was, nevertheless, thinly applied over an otherwise liberal and male-centred conception of society and human nature. Built into the poverty concept were certain liberal-individualist and familialist themes – Keynesian economic concerns about the costs of low productivity and lost output, and the liberal, middle-class touchstones of the work ethic and consumerism (e.g., see, Economic Council of Canada, 1968: 105). A mainstay of the early reports on poverty were the descriptions of the poor and their hardships in which the implicit 'other' was the middle-class individual. The hidden lesson was that poverty is the unfortunate destiny (a 'disease,' 'scourge,' or 'trap') of those who stray from a course of working, earning, and spending:

[The rural poor live] ... in the dingy squalor of the rural slum, which can be identified by ill-health, insecurity, frustration, mental and often physical in-breeding, suspicion, fear of change, and apathy. (Schlesinger, 1972: 19)

The poor do not participate in community life to the extent the more affluent groups do ... The poor are alienated from society because of society's apathy or prejudice towards the poor. (Canada, Office of the Privy Council, 1965: 7)

These persons can't plan their budgets; they have no money to plan. These figures mean that opportunity is limited. Low income can stifle initiative. Poverty breeds poverty. Of course, if you are like most Canadians, you never see these people. (Canada, Office of the Privy Council, 1967: 10–11)

The poverty concept was also imbued with a specific model of gender relations, one that supported the traditional male breadwinner family. Poverty and 'absence of male breadwinner' went hand in hand. The latter expression was used as a classification for one major group of poor in this period. The family was considered the basic decision-making unit in studies of consumption and poverty, and the male breadwinner family was the assumed model for this research – use of the 'breadwinner' term was commonplace (e.g., Canada, Minister of

National Health and Welfare, 1970; National Council of Welfare (NCW), 1971; 1973).[3] The male breadwinner was considered the main contributor to family income and the representative of the family unit. Families were classified in the data according to the characteristics of the male family head – his earnings, age, race, and so on – and it was assumed that family members pooled their incomes and resources and that women and children were under the protective wing of a male breadwinner. A tender attitude towards mother and child were, indeed, often conveyed as captured in the poetic closing to the *Statement on Income Security* of the National Council of Welfare: 'The mother and child shall have special care, for in them is the source of life and goodness. They shall receive all good things, food and air and sunlight, clothing, warmth and shelter, healing protection and love' (NCW, 1971: 33). This construction meshed with the almost hegemonic belief in the 'sanctity of the family,' a theme that was heavily promoted in the post–Second World War period by public and private social welfare agencies which were dominated by the social work profession. These agencies encouraged a belief in the fragility of the nuclear family, framing social issues in such terms as 'the problem family,' the 'deserted family,' and the 'unmarried mother.'[4] These ideas were the stuff of social security documents of the early 1970s, as in, for example, the 1973 report by the Canadian Council on Social Development (CCSD) entitled *Social Security for Canada*: 'the Task Force recognizes the importance of the family in contemporary society and stresses that social security programs should be designed so that they contribute to the successful functioning of the family,' (CCSD, 1973: 5).

All of this meant that women as 'women' were barely visible in poverty discourse in this period. Although welfare mothers were a concern from the standpoint of the number of mothers receiving welfare benefits, and they were regularly featured in the sympathy-arousing case studies of the poor, they were not primarily thought of as *women* but rather as a *welfare* problem – a point that I will return to later.[5]

If the reform agenda set by the 'rediscovery of poverty' was consistent with the qualified liberalism of the postwar era, it was also profoundly limited by the narrow 'targeting-the-poor' interpretation that it tended to promote.[6] Targeting was the fundamental objective of both CAP and the Department of Health and Welfare's 1970 white paper proposal for an income-tested family income security plan, and it was to be at the direct expense of universal measures (i.e., the Family Allowance program was to be eliminated) – although it failed to be passed in Parliament (Canada, Minister of National Health and Welfare, 1970). While the new social policy elite tended to dismiss traditional social assistance programs such as CAP as ineffective, the new model that gained popularity was, as Haddow describes, equally liberal and targeted and, I would add, sexist and familialist (Haddow, 1993: 85). The guaranteed annual income (GAI) plan advocated by the Economic Council of Canada in its 1968 annual report, by the Croll Committee, and by the Department of Health and Welfare in its 1973 orange paper (the document which set the terms of the 1973–5 federal–provincial social security review), was profoundly liberal and familialist in design: it provided for some income redistribution (all workers would receive *some* benefit) but the main emphasis was on ensuring work incentives and productivity. It would have provided just enough benefits to allow the poor to survive but at levels low enough that low wage workers (especially, male breadwinners) would have been forced into the labour market. The plan defined minimum income in terms of the 'family wage,' or amount required for the maintenance of a household composed of a husband, wife, and two children (e.g., Canada, Government of Canada, 1973; NCW, 1973). The Canadian version of the GAI was, as Haddow points out however, milder than the paradigmatically liberal U.S. plan in that it distinguished between those able and expected to work (they would receive an income supplement) and those not expected to work (they would be provided with a low level of income support). The latter would also be provided with social and employment services to help them prepare for employment. The Canadian ideal also allowed for the retention of modest universalist and insurance-based elements and comprehensive social services (Haddow, 1993; Canada, Government of Canada, 1973).

This political agenda, in turn, set the tone for a renewed social policy community and, in particular, a renewed progressive wing. While the state was relatively open to the claims of organized interest groups and movements, only *some* of the several groups and collectivities that sought a voice within the universe of discourse were able to achieve recognition as 'insiders' to the debates. Some on the political left fell into the category of 'heard, but not influential,' including, for example, the authors of *The Real Poverty Report* (1971), the renegade report of the Special Senate Committee on Poverty. In contrast to the Senate report's definition of poverty as a form of income deficiency, the *Real* report defined poverty more broadly to include inequality of power and privilege, and indicted the institutions (i.e., the media, educational system, large corporations, and unions) that legitimate power relations (McCormack, 1972; Adams, et al., 1971). Further to the margins were the neo-Marxists, including members of militant poor people's groups such as the Just Society Movement of Toronto and others who presented to the Croll Committee and who were critical of the official discourse on poverty and cynical about the attention being given to it by the ruling elite:

> Any group working within the confines of corporate capitalism must accept that political reality – that there will be no serious effort to eliminate the root condition that generates poverty – for that root condition is capitalism itself. Within these confines anti-poverty programs will continue to involve the treatment of symptoms ... To alleviate individual hardships and to dissipate social protests ... we should not be blinded by the royal commissions, task forces, new government departments and the new moral outrage against poverty that has now become so fashionable. Poverty in Canada is a product of capitalism; capitalism creates and recreates poverty. (Gonick, 1970: 8)

(Also see Buchbinder, 1970; Ford and Langdon, 1970; Canada, Senate, Proceedings of the Special Senate Committee on Poverty, 1970: (Just Society) 28: 17; Unemployed Citizens' Welfare Improvement Council, 1970.)[7]

While the labour movement was relatively strong and in a period of growth in the mid-1960s (Brodie and Jenson, 1980), its general stance towards government until the mid-1970s was adversarial and occasionally militant. Thus, its broad views of economic policy and its stand on poverty issues were accorded little attention by government (Smith, 1992; Haddow, 1993: 78). Moreover, while labour expressed sympathy for the needs of the poor, it remained somewhat ambivalent towards social assistance targeted to the poor. According to Rodney Haddow, labour 'was willing to concede to the Canadian Welfare Council (CWC) a leading role in poverty issues generally' (1993: 76–7). Women's organizations, only just emerging as a political entity in the late 1960s, early 1970s, were similarly on the margins of the social policy community, as I discuss below.

Constituencies and organizations that hewed to the social liberal targeting-the-poor reform model and were willing participants in the discourse on poverty, however, did indeed gain the recognition of state actors and began to establish a solid footing as the voice of progressives within the social policy community. At the core of this sector were three national social policy organizations (1) the federally financed, non-governmental, Canadian Welfare Council (CWC), (2) the National Anti-Poverty Organization (NAPO), and (3) the federal government's own internal National Council of Welfare (NCW). The Canadian Welfare Council had a long history as a respected contributor to social policy development in Canada. It was a meeting place for federal and provincial welfare bureaucrats in the late 1950s and 1960s, and its 1958 policy statement, entitled *Social Security for Canada*, was an important reference for Health and Welfare bureaucrats and politicians (Haddow, 1993; Splane, 1996: 42). By modernizing its structure, and changing its name to the Canadian Council on Social Development (CCSD) in 1970, the council was able to achieve greater flexibility and the research capacity needed to address the new reform agenda of the period (Haddow, 1993). The National Council of Welfare was an advisory body to the Minister of Health and Welfare. It was reorganized in 1971 in order to better fit the role of the voice of 'the poor,' albeit, under the auspices of the federal government (Haddow, 1993). Ostensibly, poor people were brought into its membership, although as Haddow points out, only 40 per cent of its members were poor. The National Anti-Poverty Organization was formed by NCW in 1971 following in the wake of a well-attended Poor People's Conference held in Toronto in January 1971.[8] While NAPO lacked the resources and expertise of the other organizations, it did have legitimacy as an organization of the poor. Its initial function was to organize the many grassroots welfare rights groups that existed at the time. Although these organizations were outside the policy-making circle and marginal to the formal social security review process, they were active in producing documents (e.g., on social security reform, the guaranteed annual income and income supplementation), organizing conferences, and providing critical commentary on government proposals. They enjoyed a relatively reciprocal relationship with federal officials, who often participated in their conferences and responded to their reports.[9] The tone of the federal response, however, seemed to vary according to the level of support these organizations gave to government proposals. For example, at a 1974 conference organized by the Canadian Council on Social Development, Health and Welfare Minister Marc Lalonde commended CCSD for its constructive advice concerning policy directions and described their relationship as a 'happy and productive' one (CCSD, 1975b: 39). A few years later, when the failure of the review loomed, Lalonde openly criticized the council, comparing it unfavourably to the National Council of Welfare, which had been more supportive of federal proposals: 'Is anybody really listening to the CCSD today? And if they are listening is the message they are getting really clear?' (CCSD, 1976b: 31). The NCW was generally held up as an authority on social security design in the mid-1970s (for example, Lalonde described NCW's *Guide to the Guaranteed Income* (1976a) as 'an invaluable short reference on the subject' (CCSD, 1976c: 31–2).

The political leanings of these organizations were indeed largely compatible with the social liberal doctrine of governmental reformers in terms of fighting poverty and achieving a more redistributive social welfare system. Like government reformers, these groups were inspired and motivated through the 1970s by the possibility of achieving a guaranteed annual income program, albeit a gentler and more generous version than the one advanced by state actors. They wanted benefit levels set to at least the poverty line, a more gradual system of recovery on earned income, and the assurance that insurance-based and some universal programs would be maintained, and employment and support services provided (CCSD, 1973; NCW, 1973). For example, their criticism of the Croll Committee's proposed GAI plan was that benefit levels were set too low (at 70 per cent of the poverty line), the recovery rate was too high (at 70 per cent on earned income) and not sufficiently graduated, and single people under age forty were not covered (NCW, 1972). They were also critical of the federal government's 1973 orange paper proposals for failing to set the minimum income at a level sufficient to bring people out of poverty and for not providing meaningful and adequate employment opportunities and social and employment services (NCW, 1973).

Beyond their watchdog role, however, these organizations performed another important public function. They furnished Canadians with the moral themes and narratives that underwrote the issue of poverty and kept it in the public eye. In the 1960s and early 1970s they generated a discourse that was grounded in the socialist Fabian tradition and drew upon the universalistic themes of international human rights discourse (e.g., the 1948 United Nations Declaration of Universal Human Rights). The Canadian Welfare Council's 1969 document, *Social Policies for Canada*, for example, was referenced to articles 22 and 25 of the 1948 U.N. declaration: 'everyone ... has the right to social security, and is entitled to realization ... of the economic, social and cultural rights indispensable for his dignity and the free development of his personality' and 'everyone has the right to a standard of living adequate for the health and well-being of himself and of his family.' The same calls for justice, equality, human rights, and dignity were reflected in the response by the National Council of Welfare to the 1970 federal white paper: 'the cornerstone of public policy in Canada today must be the recognition that the essence of a civilized society is the individual human being ... The real hope for a better Canada in the post-industrial era ... lies in the social goals of an equitable society ... The essence of this affirmation ... is commitment to the dignity and worth of human beings and their right to an equal opportunity to develop to the fullest their individual capacities ... Poverty ... is an insufficiency of income to enable full participation in the life of that society' (NCW, 1971: 1–4).

This left-liberal sector, thus, claimed a space for itself in the contemporary discussion of social policy and poverty in Canada, and it was *into* this established network and discourse of the early 1970s that second-wave feminists entered.

## Feminism, Social Policy, and the Issue of Autonomy

Women did not speak at this time as a single voice within the national social policy debate. Poor women struggled to be heard from their position within community-based welfare rights groups, of which they (along with social welfare workers) formed much of the membership (Carota, 1970). These women shared the social stigma of being single mothers on welfare and the discrimination that status entailed.[10] Groups such as Seekers of Security Welfare Rights Group Organization, Winnipeg Welfare Rights Movement (1970), Mothers on Social Allowance of Metro Winnipeg (1969), the Unemployed Citizens' Welfare Improvement Council (1970), and the Single Parents' Association of Ottawa, pleaded for attention to the situation of single mothers on welfare in briefs to the Croll Committee. They talked of being cut off benefits for sharing living quarters with a man, of having to get husbands to pay child support, and of paying for a divorce. Theirs was largely a social liberal vision based on achieving a fairer and more generous welfare system (or guaranteed annual income), including such features as the right of single mothers to earn supplementary income while on welfare, their right to receive maintenance awards without being forced to pursue estranged husbands, access to more public housing, access to subsidized day care and training, and access to legal aid or the proposition that welfare cover the cost of divorce (Canada, Senate, 1969; 1970). A continuity is, in fact, noticeable between some of these groups and those that formed in the mid- and late 1970s in Ontario to advocate on behalf of single mothers on welfare at the provincial and municipal levels, including, for example, the Family Benefits Work Group formed in the fall of 1978 (1978), the Sole Support Parents Coalition of Metro Toronto formed in the fall of 1981 (1982), the Mother's Action Group (1982), and the Mother Led Union (probably formed in the early 1980s; n.d.). The latter were responding to Ontario's move to define single mothers as 'employable' and to pressure them into the job market without the availability of adequate child care and support services (Sole Support Parents Coalition, 1982; Mother's Action Group, 1982). There was little recognition in either period, however (especially in the earlier one), of the connections between the impoverishment of welfare mothers and the broader issue of womens' subordinate social status. Few of the groups that presented to the Croll Poverty Committee appeared before the Royal Commission on the Status of Women (RCSW). Welfare mothers were for the most part perceived, and, indeed, saw themselves, as simply one of the 'minorities' that made up the population of 'the poor.' As a group they were viewed as a 'welfare issue' and 'mothers,' but not 'women':[11]

> We suggest that government must come to grips very shortly with the problems of the welfare recipient. Governments must provide us with the wherewithal to give our children a normal life ... As mothers we cannot sit idly by ... We want to do as good a job as possible and this requires a lot of outside help. (Canada, Senate, 1970: 35)

> It is of the utmost importance that we are given every consideration and help in order that we are able to fulfill our role as mothers ... we are tired of being the forgotten women at the bottom of the economic pyramid. (Mothers on Social Allowance of Metro Winnipeg, 1969: 4)[12]

One group that did bridge the gap between the issues of poverty and women's rights was the radical left poverty organization, the Just Society of Toronto. When one of the spokespersons for this group, Doris Power, spoke at a rally during the feminist Abortion Caravan campaign in May 1970 in Toronto, she did so as both a woman and a poor person: 'Many people feel that feminists are man-haters and have a lot of other equally silly notions about the Abortion Caravan. The Just Society

Movement of Toronto recognizes that the liberation of women means the liberation of men – the liberation of our society' (Power, 1972: 124).

Social and economic forces in the 1960s, including the decreasing birth rate, increasing divorce rate, and growing rate of women entering the labour force, brought an end to the norm of the one-earner family (Status of Women Canada, 1998: 7), and paved the way for the emergence of a new political movement, the second-wave women's movement. The movement was initially composed of disparate strands, reflecting radical, socialist, and liberal ideologies and interests, each seeking to shape the way we see the problems and the road to women's liberation. 'Women's liberationists' shared with the Canadian left a structural analysis of capitalism. They defined the problem in terms of women's oppression by men under capitalism: women were exploited as a cheap army of labour and given no value as mothers and homemakers. Poverty was merely a symptom of life under the capitalist, patriarchal system and could not be solved within the confines of that system: 'The only viable solutions to poverty will involve questions and answers about our taxation system, foreign investment, reclamation of Canadian resources, redistribution of wealth, control of industry, responsive government, and citizen participation ... Then one might delve into social values, the educational system, environmental control, global policy, civil rights and equal rights for women' (Spark, 1971: 5).[13]

The 'women's liberation movement' of the late 1960s and early 1970s had a stronger radical feminist bent, defining the enemy as the male chauvinist (capitalist) system that exploited women as a cheap source of labour and kept them tied to the family where they were undervalued. The welfare system was a structure that reinforced women's subservience and kept them in their roles in the family. It was as controlling a provider as a man: 'The punitive nature of the welfare system, the isolation of mothers on welfare, the dependency-reinforcement of the welfare policies, the personal degradation recipients feel, push women on welfare into a traditional role. They become agents of control and stabilizers of the social, political and economic system' (Lang, 1972: 157).[14]

While this group of feminists believed that welfare mothers needed to become conscious of their oppression as women and to organize against it, their own strategic focus was largely on working-class women and campaigns for abortion, equal pay, and child care, as well as concerns relating to unions, sexism in the media, and education (Maroney, 1987). There was one brief exception in the mid- to late 1970s, and that is the short-lived but intense campaign by the radical left (Trotskyist) group, Wages for Housework, to influence groups of welfare mothers towards achieving pay for housework.[15]

Middle-class women's associations, established during the first wave of feminism and operating primarily within an equal rights and social liberal framework, did not identify poverty as a problem for women initially. According to Florence Bird, chair of the Royal Commission on the Status of Women, poverty was one aspect of the status of women that 'all the women's groups who pushed for a Commission hadn't spent much time thinking about' (Adams, 1970: 73). These organizations tended to share the general perspective of social work in locating poverty in terms of the sociology of the family: as a problem of the 'single parent family' and 'family breakdown' (e.g., Schlesinger, 1969, 1970; Guyatt, 1971; CWC, 1968; CCSD, 1971). They were concerned especially with the financial problems of the single parent family and psychological issues created by the 'breakup of a normal family unit': 'A woman without a husband, the lone head of a household, suffers poverty in many more ways than lacking money for everyday living expenses. She suffers from the weight of responsibility on her shoulders; from loneliness; sometimes from guilt; from being "different" in a world geared to the family unit – a husband, wife and children' (Catholic Women's League of Canada, n.d.: 4).

Another key concern was the social consequences of children growing up without a male role model (e.g., Provincial Council of Women, 1970: 26; Catholic Women's League of Canada, n.d.: 4): 'children from the fatherless welfare family face a 90% chance of becoming delinquent than [sic] children who grow up in either middle class or two parent families' (Catholic Women's League of Canada, n.d.: 6). Furthermore, 'a weekly outing, with a man or senior student who would act as a substitute father, is vital to the child on welfare whose male image is negative. We therefore recommend that whatever assistance is necessary be given to ... the Big Brother Movement to provide this essential service' (ibid.: 10).

Several of these groups presented briefs on the topic of welfare mothers to the Croll Committee on Poverty, with their preferred solutions resembling those of welfare rights groups (e.g., Provincial Council of Women, 1970; the Catholic Women's League of Canada, n.d.). In presenting their briefs they were not acting primarily as political 'women' or as feminists but rather as concerned and public-minded citizens.

It was only with the issuing of the *Report of the Royal Commission on the Status of Women* in 1970 and the organizing that followed that feminists began to have an ongoing voice in the national social policy debate. The government appointed the Royal Commission on the Status of Women (RCSW) in 1967 in response to pressure by mainly white, middle-class, educated women who comprised established women's associations. The commission became a focal point for feminist mobilizing nationwide, and a large cross-section of Canadian women participated in the hearings and identified closely with the final report. The RCSW's report is generally held to be the official 'birth announcement' of the second-wave women's movement in Canada, catalyzing the organization of an important sector of the women's movement, the institutionalized women's movement, whose goal was to ensure that the government followed through on implementing the report's recommendations. It included the National Action Committee on the Status of Women (NAC),[16] a national umbrella organization that formed in 1972 and was composed mainly of liberal feminists. It also included 'status of women' groups that had emerged in several provinces, and a 'state feminist' sector composed of government-appointed bodies and a network of offices and programs within the federal public service, for example, the Co-ordinator of the Status of Women (appointed in 1970), the Minister Responsible for the Status of Women (designated in 1971), the Canadian Advisory Council on the Status of Women (CACSW; a quasi-governmental body established in 1973 whose members are appointed by government), and the Women's Program, housed in the Department of Secretary of State's Citizenship Branch (Findlay, 1987; 1988).

The RCSW process and its final report established the demure tone and narrow agenda for this sector of the women's movement well into the 1970s and 1980s. The organizations that had pushed for the commission and that formed in its wake adopted primarily a liberal 'status-of-women,' equal opportunity framework that reflected a belief in government reform and an orientation towards lobbying and consultation. They also largely accepted a universal notion of women and women's liberation that was white and middle class – although, as Jane Arscott (1977) has argued, sub-groups of women (aboriginal, poor, older, single, rural, immigrant, women with disabilities, and lesbians) are discernible on close examination of the commission's report.

The RCSW's report provided the initial blueprint as well for a feminist agenda with respect to social welfare policy. Once again its views were largely contained by the social liberal framework of Canadian reformism of this period, although it was also influenced by the variety of feminist ideologies that had a place in the broader women's movement. Social security was not addressed as a separate topic by the RCSW, yet a careful reading of the report reveals two, quite divergent, visions for reforming the social policy system. The first, reflected the relatively mainstream *liberal* side of the social liberal equation – specifically, the residual philosophy of targeting benefits only to those who have fallen through the cracks in the system. Along these lines, the commission recommended that tax exemptions (which mainly benefit the rich) be converted to tax credits in order to make the tax system more progressive and responsive to the needs of the poor. Much of the concern about poverty centred on the plights of particular vulnerable groups of women, such as single mothers, elderly women, and 'Indian,' 'Métis,' and 'Eskimo' women.[17] For example, the report recommended that the guaranteed annual income be introduced for single parent families, as a first step towards providing it for all Canadians (Canada, RCSW, 1970: 324, 302). It also supported increases to the means-tested Guaranteed Income Supplement for the elderly, and proposed the establishment of 'friendship centres' in order to ease the problems of 'Indian, Metis and Eskimo women' in adjusting to urban life (Canada, RCSW, 1970: Chapter 6).

The situation of lone mothers was seen as especially serious. The majority of single mothers were on welfare in this period and being poor and on welfare were highly stigmatized conditions, as underlined by the poverty groups presenting to the Croll Committee. This attention was also not surprising, given the new-found voices of middle-class single mothers. A new and radically different approach to single parenthood emerged with the growth and mobilization of middle-class women who had become single mothers as a result of divorce.[18] This movement was evident in the presentations to the royal commission by such community-based groups as the Minus Ones and YWCA Women Alone of Winnipeg and by recently formed status of women organizations (e.g., the Manitoba Volunteer Committee on the Status of Women, the New Brunswick Section of the Canadian Federation of University Women). These groups demanded that the single parent family be seen as a legitimate family irrespective of marital status. They framed the issue as one of discrimination and inequality: 'Society has insisted on the sole-support mother fulfilling her social and economic responsibilities even if there is no father in the home. Now society has to even the score and acknowledge the social and economic contributions she is making without recognition' (The Minus Ones, 1968: 17).

Such views represented a major shift away from the moral and psychological perspectives that had dominated the topic to this point. The solutions they advanced were for guaranteed income and assistance to allow a woman alone to become economically independent (if she chose), expanded employment opportunities, provision of upgrading courses, enforcement of minimum pay and equal pay legislation, expansion of household help, and encouragement of a child care industry. Other demands included a guarantee that child care and home help be tax deductible for single mothers, that women be exempted from paying tax on maintenance payments, that they be allowed to build up a pension in their own right whether employed or not, that marriage be seen as an economic partnership and marital property be divided equally upon divorce, and that women themselves have the final word on abortion.

Such activities and arguments were clearly an attempt by feminists to bring women and gender into the poverty discussion – a novel approach indeed given the level of silence on the issue of women's poverty within the mainstream documents of the period. As I indicated, very few of the reports of the 1960s and early 1970s on poverty addressed the topic of women's poverty (Mann, 1970; Harp and Hofley, 1971; Adams, et al., 1971).[19] The familial underpinnings of the poverty concept and the fact that the documents of the period tended to reflect the standpoint of the middle-class and elite men who thought and wrote them, meant that men were the norm within this discourse – the poor were generally depicted as men while women constituted the 'other':

> Just so long as we think of a hypothetical 'mankind' and not of individual human beings living in poverty – the very old and the very young, the distracted parents struggling for their children's food, jobless youth adrift on the streets and falling into delinquency and crime, yes – the socially inadequate who drink too much, beat their wives and children, and seem shiftless and lazy – just so long as we do not comprehend and *feel* these things, we shall fail to experience that hot human indignation that will insist on the provision of help truly geared to alleviate personal suffering. (Baetz, quoted in Robinson, 1967: 12)

> The low income person often lacks self-confidence and has a low level of self-esteem, characteristics which make him vulnerable to the blandishments of salesmen who induce him to buy by flattering his ego. He is

prone to impulse buying and vulnerable to fraud and deception. (Canadian Association of Social Workers, 1970: 7)

The odds against a child's ever lifting himself out of poverty are greater if he is raised in rural or under-developed areas rather than urban areas, and if his parents are unemployed rather than working. (Canada, Parliament, Special Senate Committee on Poverty, 1971: 39)

The poor man goes to jail far more often than the middle class lawbreaker, his sentence is usually longer. He cannot provide bail as easily, and spends more time in jail. He is ... classified more often as mentally ill and committed more frequently to public mental hospitals. He is more often taken advantage of by those whose education and training enable them to exploit him. (Baetz, 1970: 100)

Reports on poverty were, in fact, much more influenced by the politics of race (especially in the United States) and the claims of aboriginal groups and Quebec nationalism – for example, they were much more likely to focus on the poverty of 'minority' groups such as 'Eskimos,' 'Indians,' 'French-Canadians,' and 'Negroes.' If and when women were brought into the discussion, it was often for their supportive roles and sacrifices as wives and mothers, keeping their families out of poverty or stretching the unstretchable budget (e.g., 'It's a wonder how well women have been able to manage with so little, for the burden in the home usually falls on them; Canada, Parliament, Special Senate Committee on Poverty, 1971: 86).'[20] While the RCSW report might have been a force itself in penetrating such gender blindness, its approach to the issue was ultimately limited. Apart from its account of the poverty of women lacking a male partner (i.e., single mothers and elderly women), the report tended to concentrate on the subjective experience of the wife and mother living in a poor family (poverty affects all members of a family, but often it is the wife and mother who is subject to greatest stress'; Canada, RCSW, 1970: 313)). There was little or no overall understanding or evidence that welfare mothers and other groups of poor women formed a significant proportion of the poor population or that poverty was indeed a 'woman's issue.'

The second major perspective on social policy offered by the authors of the Royal Commission's report called for a more radical transformation of the social policy regime based on a 'social individual' approach. It combined aspects of social-democratic and radical feminist philosophies – a belief in the social-democratic ideals of collective provision of benefits and services and universal entitlement and a radical feminist emphasis on women's autonomy. For example, the commission supported publicly funded programs that covered broad sectors of the population and helped create a more level playing field, including for example, the established Canada/Quebec Pension Plan (C/QPP), Unemployment Insurance Programme (UI), and a progressive system of taxation. The approach was also evident in the commission's recommendations for a national, universally accessible system of day care and of homemaker services. They also advanced a belief in individual-based entitlement for social policy in keeping with the radical feminist critique of familialism (sometimes expressed as a concern about women's dependent status or their lack of autonomy within the family). This issue was at the core of the kind of feminism generally put forward by the commission and was integral to its discussion of the 'status of women.' Denying women recognition as individuals in their own right was understood as a key component of the 'discrimination' from which all women suffered: 'A woman suffers when she is not recognized as having an individual identity as a person with her own aspirations, strengths, weaknesses, tastes and ideas' (Canada, RCSW, 1970: 3). And, 'each female should be encouraged to discover her own particular gifts, talents, drives and to cultivate them for self-expression and for contribution to society' (1970: 4).

While the authors of the report distanced themselves from the radical feminist women's liberationist view that the family was the site of women's oppression (1970: 226–8), they viewed financial dependency as destructive for women (1970: 52) and criticized many social programs, particularly the more universalistic ones, for their failure to treat women as individuals. They recommended, for example, that spouses who remain at home be entitled to a pension in their own right under the Canada/Quebec Pension Plan (1970: 40), that assumptions of women's dependency be eliminated from pension plans and the UI program (1970: 82, 84), that the spouses' exemption be eliminated along with other measures that discouraged married women from entering the workforce, and that children's allowances be paid to mothers whether they worked for pay or not (1970, Chapter 5). This critique went beyond the standard liberal concept of the unencumbered individual devoid of personal and social responsibility, however (although some elements of this were indeed present). There was an implicit understanding by these actors that pursuing individual rights would help make public and visible the *social* contribution of the hidden domestic and caring labour that women did. In other words, in the particular context of the 1970s pan-Canadian social security system, wherein the principles of collective rights, universalism, and broad-based coverage were fairly well established, the demand for individual rights was seen as an important avenue for achieving recognition of the *social* importance of reproductive labour – something akin to the social individualist strategy that Winkler argues was pursued by the Swedish women's movement in the 1970s (as discussed in Chapter 1).[21]

In sum, then, it is clear that in the late 1970s the institutionalized women's movement presented a somewhat divergent and contradictory set of solutions for social policy reflecting both liberal and social-democratic impulses. On the one hand, they pushed for more money for poor women, a strategy associated with a mainstream liberal (familial and gender-blind) social policy agenda. On the other, they acted out of concern that women be treated as independent, with a right to social benefits as individuals. This reflected a desire to protect women from the vulnerabilities of dependency on husbands and families, but also, a deeper held belief that this might be a way of proceeding towards a needed fundamental change: to reconstruct domestic labour and child raising as a *social* and *public* concern and responsibility.

At least theoretically, the issue of autonomy and this thrust towards individualization presented a potential challenge to mainstream poverty-oriented social policy politics. The question to which I turn next is how did these tensions play out and how did the radical/social-democratic alternative fare? The remaining chapters will examine this issue by focusing on the political stands that feminist and other actors took in the debates of the 1980s and 1990s on federal child benefits. My findings are, perhaps, not a surprise: the ability of feminists to advance the feminist social-democratic option was constrained and ultimately diverted, and the emerging force of neo-liberalism was clearly a major explanatory factor. My focus and argument, however, concern some of the more specific mechanisms at play – that the poverty-centred claims of left-liberal organizations at the centre of the social policy community strongly conditioned the choices made by feminists. A first significant moment in the process occurred in the late 1970s' debates over child benefits, as I discuss in the next chapter.

# CHAPTER FOUR

# Feminism, Poverty Discourse, and the Child Benefits Debate of the Mid- to Late 1970s: 'Writing Women In'

Broad social and political forces, especially the declining interest in social reform and social spending, narrowed the scope for social policy debate in the mid- to late 1970s. At the same time ideological processes internal to the social policy community had an enormous influence on whether and how feminists participated in the debate. This was particularly evident in the case of child benefits policy, where two processes were important. First, poverty was constructed as a 'women's issue,' and this both gave feminists greater credibility as a voice on poverty and social security matters and encouraged a liberal turn within the women's movement that was characterized by an increasing acceptance of an 'anti-poverty' (targeting) approach to reform. Second, in the late 1970s feminists themselves took a stand on child benefits (albeit, under conditions not of their own choosing) that had consequences for pushing the issues of autonomy and individualized entitlement – along with its potential for opening up debate on private household labour – further to the political sidelines.

There were important economic and political underpinnings to these processes. Shifting trade patterns and a massive increase in the price of oil in the early 1970s contributed to an economic crisis for all advanced industrial countries. In Canada the result was upward spiralling of inflation and unemployment, a declining rate of growth, declining tax revenues, and rising public debt (Canada, Royal Commission on the Economic Union, 1985; Rice, 1985; Social Planning Council of Metropolitan Toronto, 1985). Against this background, the federal state began to retreat from 'social liberalism' in favour of *plain* liberalism. Governments lost confidence in Keynesian economics (e.g., the Trudeau government in 1978) and turned to a monetarist and supply-side doctrine of imposing high interests rates, limiting the money supply, and putting funds into the hands of private investors and entrepreneurs. Wage and price controls were introduced in 1976 and through the 1970s tax incentives were directed at the business sector. Governments began to put a new emphasis on improving relations with the business community (Rice, 1985: 241). With the election of the separatist Parti Québécois in 1976, federal attention was also diverted to questions of national unity.

This political shift corresponded to a change in relations between the state and the intermediary organizations of civil society. Faced with an attack on collective bargaining rights (i.e., wage and price controls), the labour movement was at this stage struggling to influence the political agenda. It predominantly remained, however, outside of the policymaking community (Smith, 1992). The federal state also abandoned much of its thrust in supporting interest groups. By the mid-1970s themes such as 'citizen participation' and funding possibilities for radical social movements and interest groups had come to an end (Pal, 1993). The issues of equality and social justice were not simply abandoned, to be sure. In some ways the universe of political discourse had been profoundly altered by the new social movements and interests of the 1960s and early 1970s. For example, by the mid-1970s feminism had some legitimacy and was being integrated into government agendas and discourses. Yet, governments were adopting a new passive approach to such issues. The main energies of the federal state went into containing and modifying the demands of social movements (e.g., women, native people, and multicultural groups) rather than into addressing their inequality with actual policy changes. As Suzanne Findlay comments, the state met the demands of the women's movement with a formal rather than a substantial response – by establishing advisory bodies as opposed to enacting actual policy changes (1987, 1988). Social movement organizations were having difficulty getting their issues recognized, and they were encountering ample resistance to their demands by the federal state.

By the late 1970s the first stirrings of a counter-political movement were being felt – organizations that were increasingly disappointed with the monetarist economic policy of the Trudeau Liberal government were beginning to interrelate. Common front bargaining emerged within the labour movement, and labour and community groups formed coalitions around specific issues as well more as broadly based issues and campaigns, such as peace (Bleyer, 1992: 105). These initial steps towards the formation of a popular sector network, which would concretize in the early and mid-1980s, were largely in reaction to the growing collective organization of capital, of which the 1976 formation of the Business Council on National Issues was a key moment (Bleyer, 1992: 108).

## The Broad Agenda for Social Policy

Social policy was, of course, profoundly affected by, and implicated in, these broad shifts. State actors and business interests challenged social welfare expenditures, claiming that they sapped the economic strength of the economy, siphoned off resources needed for investment, and weakened the work ethic (Rice, 1985). While federal-provincial agreement on an income supplementation plan still seemed possible in the mid-1970s,[1] by 1978 officials in the Department of Finance convinced the Liberal government that the country could not afford a guaranteed annual income program, and the social security review ground to a halt (Haddow, 1990: 224). There were strong calls for the abolishment of universal programs. The federal government, led by the Department of Finance, embarked on a new social policy agenda which prioritized the issues of cost and affordability. Greater targeting of the poor was promoted as the most cost-effective approach to poverty relief, and major cuts to social spending were announced: a three billion dollar cut in expenditures in the summer of 1978, including a reduction in the Family Allowance and Unemployment Insurance programs. As part of this package, a selective Child Tax Credit (CTC) program was introduced – it was only a pale reflection, however, of the comprehensive GAI envisioned in the early and mid-1970s (Coutts, 1992).

## Feminist Politics: Captured by Their Own Success?

Feminists were only beginning to make their mark on public consciousness and on social policy and, at least with respect to social policy, it was still very uncertain what that mark would be. Certainly, the women's movement emerged in the wake of International Women's Year (1975) with a stronger and broader base of support, more clearly defined issues (Findlay, 1987: 44), and new possibilities enabled by funding that was made available to women-related projects and to new women's organizations.[2] The 'women's state' was also rounded out with the establishment of Status of Women Canada[3] in 1976 (joining the existing

Women's Program, within the Department of the Secretary of State, and the Canadian Advisory Council on the Status of Women). A major current of the women's movement had continuing faith in government reform, sought to extend its expertise on particular issues, and tried to develop lobbying skills and establish a more collaborative and consultative footing with government (Findlay, 1988: 7). Findlay has argued that liberal feminism became the 'public face' of the women's movement at this time, although according to Vickers et al. (1993), the National Action Committee's umbrella structure (an organization that represented a wide array of women's groups) allowed for the participation of socialist and radical strains.[4] In any case, the women's movement was struggling in this period to place women's issues on the political agenda and to achieve real policy changes. Organizations such as NAC and the CACSW were presenting positions on a wide range of issues affecting women's equality and trying to put forward new policy demands that moved feminism beyond the recommendations of the Royal Commission on the Status of Women (Findlay, 1988). They focused in particular on such areas as pensions, equal pay for work of equal value, rape, wife battering, divorce reform, affirmative action, child care, and birth-control services (Findlay, 1988: 7; Vickers et al., 1993: 83). As Findlay comments of this period, however, 'while our commitment to equality was strong, our expertise did not yet match our enthusiasm' (1988: 6). NAC was indeed having difficulty organizing itself to advance a truly national perspective, and its membership suffered from an underrepresentation of working-class, native, immigrant, and lesbian women (ibid.). The CACSW, for its part, had little credibility with the wider women's movement, although it did have the advantage of an independent research capacity, greater access to inside information on government initiatives, and a good working relationship with NAC (Vickers, et al., 1993: 83; Monica Townson, personal interview).[5]

While social security and poverty were still relatively minor issues for these organizations, a handful of their researchers and policy analysts did have a commitment to social policy issues and had expertise to formulate positions in the areas of taxation and social security.[6] Indeed, the concern that women receive individual treatment under social programs – with the focus most often being on core federal, broad-based programs – was one of the driving forces behind their efforts. Feminist researchers such as Margrit Eichler and Brigitte Kitchen, who were outspoken on this issue in the late 1970s and early 1980s, helped to establish these ideas as fundamental feminist principles (Eichler, 1980, 1983b; 1983c; Kitchen, 1980, 1984). Eichler was a particularly ardent critic of family-based social programs. As she pointed out, family income is 'too crude an indicator to tell us much about the disposable income of individuals who make up so-called "economic families"' inasmuch as not all members of the family have equal access to the family's resources (1980: 20). She forcefully argued for making the individual, and not the family, the administrative unit for social programs ('always and under all circumstances'; 1983b: 126).

The concern was often raised in relation to a range of social programs which were seen to assume women's dependence (whether it be that women's work was of lesser value, or did not count, or that their access to paid labour was of lesser importance than men's). One of the clearest articulations of the position was by the CACSW. It recommended that women should be treated as deserving the protection of social security and pension benefits in their own right based on their own work, and not just indirectly or as derivative of their husbands' rights (based on their paid work; CACSW, 1976b: 13). The council's goal was to achieve recognition for 'women as individuals with economic responsibilities towards themselves and towards their dependents,' and it called for a realignment of social security such that the focus would be the individual and not the family unit (1974: 3; 1976b: 13). The approach implied a rejection of the traditional family model – a model that, as one author put it, 'disguises the position of the woman in the family and attributes to her a degree of security she does not have. It disguises the fact that the major part of the work women do makes no contribution to their economic security, rather actually inhibits it. Too many women, after a lifetime of work on behalf of their families and society, find themselves alone and practically or actually destitute. Their protection is dependent on good will and good luck, not on good law or good social policy, or on their own economic contribution over the years' (1976b: 11; also, 1976a: 34).

This criticism was also voiced through the mid-1970s in relation to pensions (CACSW, 1974). The spousal allowance component of the Canada Pension Plan, for example, was considered to be giving 'credence to the idea that the proper place for a woman was to be dependent upon a man' (1979: 2). CPP survivor benefits were also criticized for not treating male and female contributors equally and for stipulating that widows lose their benefits if they remarried (CACSW, 1979; *Status of Women News*, 1977). The 'pensions for homemakers' debate that emerged within the movement in the early 1980s was also in some sense a reflection of this autonomy-within-collectivism thrust. While there were differences of opinion over the design of such a program, there was ample agreement about the objective – to provide women with a pension in their own right and as recognition of their household labour. Proponents were assuming that this would occur within the auspices of, or alongside, a generous universalistic pension plan. This issue was also raised, of course, in relation to provincial social assistance programs, whose sexist 'spouse in the house' rule was noted in the early 1970s (Zuker and Callwood, 1971) and would come under sustained fire in the mid-1980s.[7]

The institutionalized women's movement (especially NAC and CACSW) became ever more attuned to the issue of autonomous treatment as proposals surfaced in the mid- and late 1970s that threatened women's independent right to some core benefits. For example, the federal Department of Finance expressed renewed interest in 'joint' taxation, an idea that the Carter Commission (1966) and, indeed, the RCSW, had earlier recommended. Feminists denounced this plan for its likely effect of discouraging married women from returning to work and for falsely assuming that family members always share their incomes (CACSW, 1976a: 31; 1977a; 1978a).[8] The position that emerged within the institutionalized women's movement did have a particularly 'liberal feminist' flavour, to be sure, in its preoccupation with achieving equity within marriage and the family: 'until Canadian women enjoy full economic equality within marriage, no measures should be introduced to erode the independent financial status now provided' (NAC, 1978a: 7).[9] Feminists of all persuasions viewed federal proposals to base UI benefits on family income as a threat to women's independent access to benefits. As a spokesperson for NAC put it, '[this] would in effect ... deny married women the right to participate in the labour force on the same terms and conditions as everyone else. We have a Human Rights Act which forbids discrimination in employment on the grounds of sex and marital status' (NAC, 1978b: 17).[10]

Likewise, feminists in and around formal women's organizations (both socialist- and liberal-minded) strongly rejected the Conservative government's 1979 proposal to give higher UI benefits to recipients with dependents. With most married women earning income well below their husbands, a two-tier system would disproportionately deny benefits to married women (Townson, 1980; Eichler, 1980; Kitchen, 1980). Thus, the importance of basing UI benefits on individual rather than family attachment to the labour force was a constant refrain in the resolutions passed by CACSW and NAC (*Status of Women News*, 1980; CACSW, 1980b). The Family Allowance Programme also came under attack by the federal government, which reduced it in the late 1970s and then threatened to eliminate it completely (i.e., the Conservatives in December 1979 and the Liberals in the fall of 1982). Feminists argued (as they had done in the case of joint taxation) that until there was equitable sharing of family resources it would be wrong to take the allowance away from women on the basis of their husband's income (e.g., NCW, 1979a, 1983). The 'universality versus selectivity' question, which emerged in a somewhat abstract form in the late 1970s, was also viewed from this vantage point by feminists of all casts.[11] They supported universality for social-democratic / class solidarity reasons, but also because of the potential that universal benefits and services presented for recasting domestic work from a private to a public and social concern and for giving women benefits in their own name. Selectivity was viewed, on the other hand, as reinforcing private responsibility and increasing women's dependency on the family (CACSW, 1980a; 1982; Townson, 1980). By the early 1980s there was even a willingness among some left-liberal social policy analysts to look inside the 'black box' of the family unit to ask questions about the distribution of income therein (e.g., CCSD, 1981; Moscovitch, 1982; Shifrin, 1980).

This thread of analysis – this defamilialized, and often, social individualist model – would never fully flower, however, into a more encompassing challenge to the liberal mindset dominating the social policy system. Notwithstanding the above interventions, it appears indeed that the women's movement was inexorably drawn towards a liberal-familial worldview centred on the issue of poverty. As discussed earlier, feminists had long recognized that women made up a good proportion of the 'working poor' and those on social assistance and had from the beginning expressed concern about poverty and made recommendations for addressing it. They had called, for instance, for a fairer tax system and for an adequate allowance for families with children. A 1976 report on women and taxation, written by Louise Dulude for the CACSW, reiterated the importance for women and the poor of replacing tax *exemptions* (especially the children's exemption) with tax *credits* (CACSW: 1976a). The CACSW and NAC had issued almost identical recommendations to this effect in the mid-1970s on the grounds of equitability between the rich and poor (CACSW, 1978b: 4; Status of Women News, 1976: 6; 1977: 10). By the late 1970s women's organizations were indeed aligned with anti-poverty organizations in calling for an 'income support and supplementation' plan to ensure an adequate guaranteed income for all Canadians (*Status of Women News*, 1978). They also joined with social policy organizations in supporting the targeted, (family) income-tested Child Tax Credit Programme, which they viewed as a step towards abolishing tax exemptions – again, something for which they had long called.[12]

That this shift occurred is perhaps easiest understood as a response to the changing social, economic, and political climate towards the end of the decade. This new climate included a growing acceptance of a residual role for the state in social policy and a growing intolerance for what had begun to be viewed as costly ideals – for example, equality, individuality, and autonomy. But to explain the changes entirely in terms of broad macro-level forces leaves out an important, more subtle, level of activity and struggle and misrepresents the processes involved. Indeed, the more specific ideological context within the smaller world of the social policy community – a world in which social policy organizations largely defined progressive ideals for social policy – also had a profound influence on feminist thinking. A significant factor was the way the notion of poverty was being reformulated as a gendered matter.

### Progressive Actors and the Emerging Focus on 'Women and Poverty'

Beyond the realm of government and business, certain progressive groups did continue to have more credibility than others in influencing the national debate on social policy. The labour movement was not one of them. Labour maintained a position at the periphery of the progressive-liberal social policy community. Preoccupied with the issues of unemployment, cuts in social spending, and wage and price controls, organized labour did not have a firm view on the GAI proposal that dominated the discussion during the mid-1970s social security review. It neither opposed nor promoted this plan, although in the latter half of the decade it did champion the reform of the CPP (Haddow, 1994; Myles, 1988a). The Canadian Labour Congress advanced a social-democratic position, which saw full employment as the first defence against poverty, supplemented by adequate minimum wage legislation, strong labour market and manpower [sic] policies, and regional development. Universal and insurance-based measures (UI, CPP, Old

Age Security, family allowances, sickness and maternity benefits) were considered a second defence, while the GAI was seen as a program of last resort (Haddow, 1994: 171). Although the women's movement was becoming more influential in national politics generally, it, too, was a marginal political actor within the national social policy debate.

The positioning of these actors contrasted markedly with that of national, left-liberal, social policy organizations (predominantly, CCSD, NCW, and NAPO) who continued to occupy a more privileged position as the voice of progressives on social policy issues and to play a supportive role on the sidelines of the social security review. In response to the growing worry about social spending, these organizations strengthened their call for eliminating the income gap between the rich and poor (CCSD, 1973; NCW, 1973). The issues of poverty and income disparity between the rich and poor remained touchstones for these organizations through the late 1970s and early 1980s (e.g., CCSD, 1979a, 1979b, 1981). While some factions within this sector grew more willing to support greater targeting (i.e., selectivity) of the system, the pattern for the most part was to continue to cite the advantages of 'universality' over 'selectivity' (CCSD, 1979a; Shifrin, 1978b). For example, a key issue for the National Council of Welfare in the late 1970s was the elimination of tax exemptions (which gave greater benefits to the rich and high-income earners) and the adoption of a system of refundable tax credits for poor and low-income families with children (NCW, 1978; Shifrin, 1978c). The selective Child Tax Credit introduced in 1978 was viewed by these players as an important advance in the design of social programs and as potentially prefiguring their ideal of a full 'income support and supplementation' plan delivered through the tax system (Shifrin, 1978c: 12).

Again, while these organizations had little direct influence on actual policy-making, they played a powerful role in shaping Canadian views on poverty and compassion. With a view to bolstering public interest in reforming the social security system, one of the key activities of this sector in the mid-1970s was to renew and rework the issue of poverty. Indeed, over the course of the 1970s these organizations gained a reputation as poverty experts. They developed and distributed a substantial body of material on poverty, much of which were compilations and analyses of the data. The Canadian Council on Social Development's 'fact books on poverty' were a prime example. Mainly written by CCSD's leading analyst, economist David Ross (who would later become its executive director), the fact books became a definitive reference on the current state of poverty, selecting and interpreting data compiled by Statistics Canada (the latter of which continued as the 'official' voice on poverty).[13] The National Council of Welfare also began in the early 1980s to publish a series of statistical reports on poverty and the technicalities of poverty lines. For poverty to remain a viable public policy issue and to attract sympathy for the poor, however, statistics were not enough – poverty had to have a human face. To this end, CCSD, and more particularly the NCW, began to produce material that focused on the plight of especially vulnerable groups – that is, single parents, children, women, and poor families (NCW, 1975, 1976b, 1979a). These reports served to provide a venue for their commentary on the most recent government proposal and were a tool for maintaining the pressure on policymakers.[14]

They were also a primary instrument in 'writing women in' to the poverty problem. Indeed, several documents released during the period of the mid-1970s to early 1980s highlighted the special problems of women. They included, for example, *One in a World of Twos* (NCW, 1976b), *Women in Need – A Source Book* (CCSD, 1976c), *Women and Pensions* (Collins, 1978), *Women and Poverty* (NCW, 1979a), *In the Best Interests of the Child* (NCW, 1979b), and *Women and Housing* (McClain and Doyle, 1984). These reports were in many ways *feminist* documents – they reflected the new legitimacy that the identity 'women' and 'women's issues' had gained by this time. They emphasized the difficulties that women faced in trying to earn an independent living ('The odds are stacked against them from the start.'; NCW, 1976b: 6), owing to discrimination in the labour market, pay inequality, occupational segregation, and so on. While national social policy organizations, including especially CCSD and NCW, were largely controlled and staffed by male social policy analysts, feminist researchers, writers, and consultants were hired for specific projects, including, for example, Louise Dulude (of NAC and CACSW) for the NCW's *Women and Poverty*, Suzanne Findlay (of the CACSW) and various others for CCSD's *Women in Need* and *Women and Housing* projects. The NCW's report, *Women and Poverty*, written by Dulude, was typical of this genre of publication, and it was a key document in putting gender on the poverty map.[15] According to Dulude, poverty research and analysis had had a strong male bias up to this point: poverty was largely explained in terms of unemployment and the 'culture of poverty.' She maintained that much of the poverty in Canada was because women were raised with the expectation that they would be financially supported for life by men, and, moreover, that this explanation 'might have been arrived at long ago if poverty experts had not ignored the fact that so many of the poor are female' (NCW, 1979a: 2).[16] According to her report, women's poverty flowed from their inequality in education, in employment, in marriage (having most of the responsibility for raising children), and because of marriage breakdown.

As the latter variable hints, the central figure in this new poverty discourse was the single mother. Indeed, the single-parent mother was positioned in this material as exemplifying not only women's poverty, but the *general* problem of poverty. The focus on single mothers clearly reflected a new material reality taking shape at this time, namely, fundamental shifts in family structure. The continuing decline in the birth rate (which peaked in 1976 and then levelled off) and the increase in women's labour force participation (which roughly went from 40 per cent of women in 1971 to over 50 per cent by 1981; CACSW, 1990a) meant that the dual-earner family was quickly replacing the single male-breadwinner as the predominant family type in Canada.[17] With the divorce rate accelerating (rising by 82 per cent between 1972 and 1982; MacDaniel, 1993: 113), the number of single-parent families also rose in relation to those with two parents (going from 9 per cent of families in 1971 to 11 per cent in 1981; Status of Women Canada, 1986: 12), and many of these were headed by women and living in poverty.[18] Thus, one of the major new poverty themes to emerge was that of the poverty of the single-earner (usually single-parent) family relative to the dual-earner family, with the implicit 'other' being the affluent two-earner family which by the late 1970s was becoming the norm. Another emerging theme was that the increased participation of women in employment was protecting many families from falling into poverty (CCSD, 1983: 20).

This discourse was also *socially constructed*, however. It was, indeed, a collaboration between core social policy and anti-poverty and liberal feminist actors. Liberal feminism advanced a politicized view of single motherhood through the mid-1970s in which the conditions of this status were seen to reflect women's overall subordinate and oppressed condition (a view first evident in a strand of presentations to the RCSW, as discussed earlier).[19] Government documents of the early and mid-1970s also began to reflect these ideas. For example, while the breadwinner family was still primarily the norm and 'the family' ideal still considered sacrosanct,[20] gender-neutral language and the idea of giving single mothers greater 'choice' under income support plans began to be adopted. The 1973 federal orange paper, for example, allowed single mothers to earn income while receiving welfare benefits and ensured the provision of income supplementation and day care in order to encourage them to take training or upgrading to enhance their employability (Canada, Government of Canada, 1973: 20). Feminist ideas about single mothers – especially the notion that they are 'deserving' – also became central components of the new conception of women's poverty. Single mothers were presented as victims of the discrimination and injustice that all women faced – victims of structural forces beyond their control (e.g., the increasing divorce rate) and of traditional socialization patterns: 'The reality is that most didn't *plan* to be single parents; circumstances along the way caused them to be widowed, divorced, deserted, whatever' (NCW, 1976b: 12). They were cast as responsible parents, even heroes, raising their families despite the odds against them, and deserving of society's respect and support.

Feminists' growing involvement through the decade in the issues of redistribution and poverty was clearly underwritten by this flourishing belief that poverty was a women's issue. The publication of the NCW's *Women and Poverty*, for example, furnished women's groups with new political leverage for making demands on behalf of women, which again, further drew feminists into discussions of poverty, social security, redistribution, and the like.[21] Feminsts gained an important new framing strategy, something that was apparent, for example, in their calls in the early 1980s for inclusion of homemakers in the Canada Pension Plan: 'The poverty facing old and retired women ... is a crisis, a national shame. We recommend radical solutions to solve radical problems. We ask for whatever measures are necessary to increase the current income of elderly women so that those living below the poverty line will be able to end their years in dignity' (NAC, 1981: 7).[22] For the first time since *Report of the Royal Commission on the Status of Women*, feminist organizations began again to focus on women's poverty, for example, the CACSW published a 'fact sheet' on women and poverty (CACSW, n.d., *Women and Poverty*).

Of course, this construction also profoundly influenced a feminist perspective on social policy. The view that it encouraged was that women had much to gain from an expansion of anti-poverty measures, especially those that targeted the most vulnerable of families, namely, those led by single mothers. Nowhere was this more obvious than in the late 1970s' debate on the Child Tax Credit (CTC). This debate marked a critical moment in the reconciliation of competing feminist visions for social policy, and it was indeed a turning point for institutionalized feminism in terms of choosing to favour (family-based) programs targeted to the poor over other options. The CTC was introduced as part of a package of spending cuts that included a significant reduction of the universal Family Allowance – a step that was held to be necessary in order to fund the new credit. Feminists 'deeply regretted' the reduction of the Family Allowance (they were in fact 'furious,' according to one participant). In announcing its approval of the CTC, the National Action Committee on the Status of Women reiterated its call for the government to abolish the children's exemption and, with the funds thereby saved, to increase the Family Allowance (to a level higher than it was before the cut; Louise Dulude, personal interview). This choice was clearly a pragmatic one – the CTC was viewed as the most progressive measure that could be achieved at the time given the situation of retrenchment, of fragile federal–provincial relations vis-à-vis social programs, and the general level of hostility towards social spending and universality. The response was also filtered, however, through the established lens of 'women and poverty,' with its dictum that 'what is good for the poor, is good for women' – especially lone-mother families. The needs of the latter were indeed foremost at this time in the minds of the individual feminists involved. For example, this thinking was reinforced by federal Minister of Health and Welfare Monique Bégin when she introduced the legislation. Bégin, who had also been privy to debates within the RCSW, consistently stressed the particular advantages that she believed the program would have for single-parent mothers.[23] She made much of the fact that the · Child Tax Credit would be paid to *women* despite the fact that it was first and foremost a tax offset for higher earning spouses (generally husbands).[24]

Examining the debates surrounding this legislation more closely, it is clear that the issue of individual entitlement was never, in fact, broadly debated. Flora MacDonald (a 'Red Tory' and Conservative critic of the new legislation) attempted to stir controversy when she argued that the CTC really amounted to 'joint taxation' and would thus act in a similar way to deter women from participation in the labour force and, indeed, threaten their economic independence (Canada, House of Commons, 1978: 756–9; 1684–7; *Globe and Mail*, 1978). The responses of women's organizations were shaped primarily, however, by the liberal feminist experts on income security issues within NAC and CACSW, backed up by key figures within the Liberal Party. These feminists were not convinced of the 'radical feminist' position that all social programs should be based on individual entitlement (e.g., Dulude, 1979: 10). They viewed this as unreasonable and impractical under the circumstances, and not in keeping with the immediate interests of the most vulnerable women (ibid.; Canada, House of Commons Debates, 1978: 1629). Both Dulude and Bégin shared the view, for instance, that the principle of women's financial autonomy is not relevant with respect to social security programs geared to the poor. They reasoned that since poor households spend all their income on necessities (all income is *shared* in this sense), the question of who has the power in the family is not relevant. In Dulude's words, 'When a family spends its entire income on basic necessities, it does not make sense to say that the husband or the wife has decision-making power over spending and saving choices, because there are in fact no such choices to be made. Social security programs aimed at ensuring that people's basic needs are met are therefore accurate in their assumption that their client-families share everything they own' (Dulude, 1979: 10).

Likewise, according to Bégin, 'In lower middle class and poor families women and husbands work together. Each knows what the other earns. Their money is put together. There never is enough money. The economic autonomy which is the symbol of some women's movements happens only in rich social classes. In those classes wives do not work outside, and husbands do not give their wives enough of their salaries. That is not what happens in poor families and in the lower middle classes' (Canada, House of Commons Debates, 1978: 1986).

The strategy of individualizing benefits also competed in this case with another important liberal feminist goal, namely, that of achieving a greater sharing of the burdens and responsibilities of parenting. As Brigitte Kitchen argued, 'If we accept that children are the joint responsibility of both their parents, it does not seem out of place to expect the income of both parents to be considered in determining eligibility. If only the mother's income were considered, as is the case in mother-led one-parent families, the implicit policy implications would be that children are primarily the responsibility of their mothers, and not of both their parents' (Kitchen, 1979: 49, 50).

Bégin advanced similar arguments in parliamentary debate: 'For years women have been fighting to get fathers to assume parenthood with them jointly. They do not want to be left alone to solve problems, to provide care and to take responsibility for their children ... *When it comes to children we cannot speak of autonomy of women as opposed to men.*

*This is not the forum for that.* We want two parents to be responsible for their children and to exercise their responsibility jointly' (Canada, House of Commons Debates, 1978: 30 Nov., 1686; my emphasis).

With this thinking and policy choice, feminists within the institution-alized movement showed unwillingness to apply the individualization strategy with a broad brush across the social policy field. In effect, they deemed it to be applicable only to particular, long-standing, universal-type programs that were thought to have 'symbolic significance' for women in seeming to recognize the work of child raising that they performed and in providing them with benefits in their own name – that is, the Family Allowance and Old Age Security programs (Dulude, 1979). In effect, feminists opted for a dual strategy for achieving a women-friendly income support system: on the one hand, the goal was to secure more generous benefits for single mothers through a liberal strategy of family-based and targeted programs, and on the other, they left open the door to continue to press for a 'social individual' vision by seeking individualized benefits under universalistic programs, espe-cially the Family Allowance. With respect to the allowance, however, a benefit that women had always received without question of their husband's income, the position advanced at the end of the 1970s – that *both* personal and family income should be taken into account – was far short of the purely individual entitlement approach preferred by radi-cal and socialist feminists (CACSW, 1980).

The mid- to late 1970s was a critical period, then, with respect to shaping 'women's interests' within the federal social security field, especially in the playing out of the tensions between the social indi-vidual versus anti-poverty approach. Major influences came from both broad political conditions and discursive constructions within the 'policy community.' Feminists were successful in penetrating the gender-blind construction of the poverty problem – something that was an accom-plishment in and of itself, and one that made much greater space for a feminist voice within the debate on social policy. At the same time, however, their political choices entailed losses and contradictions, the implications of which may not have been fully appreciated by the actors of the day. First, the discourse on women and poverty was essentially a narrow, liberal reading of women's poverty that fitted the terms of the dominant familialist paradigm. Missing from the account was the view that poverty was a problem for women in general, inde-pendent of family relationships, and as a consequence of their low wages and an independent income. Also eclipsed were broader, radical, and socialist perspectives that connected poverty to capitalist and patriarchal structures. Second, feminist gains came at the expense of a broader vision for social policy entailed in the social individual alternative, an alternative that promised a more fundamental challenge to the dependency and poverty of women. In hindsight, it is clear that this was only the beginning of a neo-liberal transition in which targeted programs would replace universal ones, and for which the focus on the problem of poverty, and the political choices of social policy and feminist activists to support greater targeting, only helped pave the way.

The next chapter describes some of the more immediate consequences of these events. Having traded off the Family Allowance and the principle of autonomy for a GAI-type program, feminists were not in a strong position to defend the allowance when it came under attack again – but, again, there were multiple influences conditioning their choices.

# CHAPTER FIVE

# Feminism and the Tory Child Benefits Debate of the Early to Mid-1980s: Money in Their Own Name?

A second conjunctural moment in the shaping of feminist approaches to social policy occurred in the mid-1980s as the women's movement waged the battle to defend women's individual entitlement to benefits and to protect Family Allowance benefits. These related causes lost much of their momentum, however, in the mid-1980s. A key point in this process occurred as the institutionalized women's movement opted to support rather than challenge the Tory agenda on family and child benefits policy. In making this decision feminists were clearly taking into account major new influences of the day – most emphatically, an overarching neo-conservative agenda that sought to reduce and re-structure the social policy system. Less obvious, perhaps, but equally important influences in these matters were left-liberal social policy organizations that had been feminists' allies within the social policy community. Specifically, the narrow and defensive stance taken by these groups in mounting opposition to neo-conservative plans for child benefits created a further barrier to feminists contemplating advancing within this debate the notion of individualized rights, with its underlying support for social recognition and responsibility for care work.

Canada entered a severe recession in 1981–2, which was followed by slow and hesitant growth. These trends were the reflection of deep structural changes, including low productivity growth, technological change that transformed the occupational structure, and increasing competition in international trade (Banting, 1987a). Economic problems continued to create what came to be called a fiscal crisis for the state and contribute to a substantial level of government debt. Unemployment peaked at about 12 per cent in 1983 (up from 7.5 per cent in 1980) and then gradually decreased until the recession of the late 1980s. The shift towards globalization of production and neo-conservative policies (e.g., free trade with the United States) led to a restructuring of employment and a trend towards an increasing proportion of low-paid, part-time, and service-sector jobs. Part-time work grew in importance and was increasingly filled by people who would have preferred full-time work, and there was a rapid increase in the numbers of people dependent on government social programs and private charity (Banting, 1987b).

While many features of neo-conservative economic policy were initiated by the Trudeau Liberals in the late 1970s and early 1980s (e.g., monetarism, a tight money supply, the introduction of the '6 and 5' anti-inflation policy, and public spending cuts), the Mulroney government, elected in 1984, was even more committed to controlling the deficit, reducing government expenditures, and encouraging market forces and the private sector through such strategies as tax restructuring, privatization, and deregulation (Rice and Prince, 1993: 411). The centrepiece of its economic agenda was negotiating a free trade agreement with the United States. This economic strategy was also accompanied by a wave of neo-conservative ideology that advocated a return to patriarchal family values and practices. For example, the Mulroney government's 'Family Caucus' (a group of thirty-five social-conservative MPs who held seats in the federal Tory government) was committed to upholding and enhancing the single male-breadwinner family (Bashevkin, 1998; Luxton, 1997).

This shift towards neo-conservatism was matched by changes in the broader political terrain. The adoption of an explicitly neo-conservative/neo-liberal economic agenda gave rise to an oppositional movement in civil society that would have a marked influence on the universe of political discourse throughout the period of the Mulroney government. The election of this government and the process and final report of the Macdonald Commission (which was in step with the Mulroney economic agenda) created a clear demarcation between the neo-conservative corporate vision of Canada, also supported by business organizations, 'think tanks' like the Fraser Institute, the Economic Council of Canada (ECC), the C.D. Howe Institute (Porter, 2003), and a growing 'popular sector' perspective (Bleyer, 1992: 105). Through the early and mid-1980s a range of groups representing labour, women, the church, and farmers formed relationships and joined coalitions to oppose the free trade deal. The most significant of these were the Council of Canadians (formed in 1985) and the Pro-Canada Network (initiated in April 1987), made up of dozens of national organizations such as the Canadian Labour Congress (CLC), NAC, the National Farmers' Union, and Gatt-Fly, as well as provincial coalitions against free trade. With the concretization of the free trade deal in the fall of 1987, and the emergence of a powerful lobby for business, the Pro-Canada Network became more active in advancing an alternative economic agenda and broadening its mandate to counter the neo-conservative/neo-liberal agenda. It was especially prominent in challenging the free trade deal and the Mulroney government in the 1988 election, and it continued into the 1990s to oppose neo-liberalism and to promote an alternative economic vision.

The relationship that had been established between the federal government and non-governmental interest groups would also begin to fray beginning in the mid-1980s as the Mulroney government (abetted by the Reform Party and the right wing) began to question the practice of funding organized interest groups. In 1986–7, the Tories began to selectively cut grants and contributions to groups – not least to women's and Aboriginal organizations (Jenson and Phillips, 1996: 123). The funding practices of the Women's Programme came under scrutiny at this time, primarily instigated by REAL Women, a right-wing, anti-feminist group that was particularly interested in challenging the funding base of NAC, Canada's largest national feminist organization. The question of funding women's organizations came under review beginning in January 1987, and REAL Women was granted funding by the Secretary of State at the end of 1988. The Women's Programme budget was finally frozen in February 1989, and substantial cuts to its budget would follow through the 1990s, which would mean significant reductions to NAC's budget in particular (Pal, 1993: 143–8; Vickers et al., 1993: 146–8).

### The New Neo-Conservative Parameters for Social Policy

The federal Tories' main priority for social policy was achieving reductions in social spending, primarily through targeting the truly needy. In fact, its first-term social policy agenda did not break sharply with that of the previous Liberal government. The Liberals had emphasized spending reductions, helping those 'most in need' (e.g., reducing the indexation of Old Age Security Pensions and Family Allowances) and had opened up 'for debate' the ending of the universality of the Family Allowance (as reflected in remarks by Finance Minister Marc Lalonde in November 1982). The Liberals had also failed to respond to the call by social policy activists, women's organizations, and labour groups during 'the great pension debate' of the early 1980s to expand the pension system (Myles, 1988a).[1] What was different with the arrival of the Conservative government, however, was its promise from the outset to focus on reforming social policy and of the possibility of major changes to programs. Indeed, over the course of the 1980s the Tories put a large number of social programs on the table, including transfer payments to the provinces for health and post-secondary education, Unemployment Insurance, elderly benefits (i.e., Old Age Security, the Guaranteed Income Supplement, the Canada Pension Plan), family and child benefits (i.e., the Child Tax Credit, Family Allowance, and Child Tax Exemption programs), and taxation. A new policy environment emerged in the mid-1980s as a result of the many substantial reform proposals put forward by several federal and provincial commissions and task forces that reported at this time. Federally, the Royal Commission on the Economic Union and Development Prospects for Canada (the Macdonald Commission, originally established by the Trudeau government) proposed a comprehensive GAI-modelled plan to replace the existing range of programs, the Commission of Inquiry on Unemployment Insurance (the Forget Commission) proposed a major restructuring and downsizing of the UI program, and the Task Force on Child Care recommended massive restructuring and expansion of day care services (Canada, Royal Commission on the Economic Union and Development Prospects for Canada, 1985; Canada, Commission of Inquiry on Unemployment Insurance, 1986; Status of Women Canada, 1986). Provincially, the Newfoundland Report of the Royal Commission on Employment and Unemployment proposed a GAI for its province, and the Ontario Report of the Social Assistance Review Committee proposed a major overhaul of Ontario's social assistance system (Newfoundland Royal Commission on Employment and Unemployment, 1986; Ontario Social Assistance Review Committee, 1988).

Another feature that distinguished this era was that policy-making in social policy was placed entirely in the hands of the Department of Finance, and there was little pretense of involving other key departments such as Health and Welfare. Rodney Haddow reports that by the late 1980s, Finance's Social Policy Division had become an active policy-maker in its own right, 'concentrating on the potential use of the tax system as a mechanism for meeting social policy objectives ' (1990: 231). The Tories briefly resurrected the idea of extensive and open consultation, especially in the area of social policy, although, as analysts would later note, 'reality fell far short of the rhetoric' (Phillips, 1991: 190).[2] The government invited the public and a wide variety of interest groups to participate in a 'frank and open' discussion about the role of social programs (Rice, 1987: 216). It issued 'consultation' papers (e.g., Child and Elderly Benefits in 1985) which outlined 'options.' It established numerous sets of House of Commons and Senate Committee hearings that provided a venue for debate,[3] and it conducted regular pre-budget consultations with various interest groups. The terms of the consultations and debates, however, were carefully orchestrated by the Department of Finance who decided which program areas would be reviewed, what the fiscal parameters for reform would be, what the venues would be, and how much time would be allowed for debate.

The broad agenda for social policy, presented by the Department of Finance in September 1984, reinforced the language of targeting the 'truly needy,' with the claim that this would achieve more socially and fiscally 'responsible' social programs: 'wherever possible, and to a greater extent than is the case today, scarce resources should be diverted first to those in greatest need' (Canada, Minister of Finance, 1984: 71); and 'government expenditures must be allocated to provide immediate employment opportunities and better ensure sustained income growth' (ibid.). This ethos was reflected in the widely quoted query by Prime Minister Mulroney at this time: 'Are we making proper use of the taxpayers' money by giving bank presidents who make $500,000 a year a baby bonus? Could that money not be more properly used to assist someone who desperately needs help?' (*Status of Women News*, 1985: 2). The thrust reflected a return to a 'residual' philosophy emphasizing individual initiative and private responsibility for social and economic well-being and greater acceptance of private charity such as food banks (which were proliferating). This thinking was also reflected in the Macdonald Commission's proposals for social security which advocated incentives 'to encourage people to take advantage of their opportunities' (Canada, Royal Commission on the Economic Union, 1985: 15), 'improve their own situation' (1985: 16), and 'take responsibility for their own lives and livelihood when they are able to do so' (1985: 15). According to the commission, income security programs 'impair incentives for individuals to improve their own situation and ... must provide incentives that will encourage "employable" beneficiaries to try to find employment, participate in job-training and skills upgrading programs, make appropriate use of occupational and geographic mobility, and form stable work attachments' (1985: 16). Its proposals were based on distinctions between the 'deserving' and 'undeserving,' which it defined according to length of attachment to the labour market – less stable, shorter-attachment workers were defined as less deserving than longer-attachment workers. This philosophy had a particular gender inflection as well. 'The family' was extolled as the basic unit of society: 'Particular care must ... be taken not to build into income-security programs incentives which may diminish family formation or lead to breakdowns in family structure' (Canada, Royal Commission on the Economic Union, 1985: 17).

The underlying assumption was that of the *dual*-breadwinner family, however, consisting of *deserving* (male) primary workers and *undeserving* (female) secondary workers.[4] First-class benefits would be provided to primary family earners and second-class (lower) benefits to secondary earners. The scheme assumed that when in need, secondary ('unstable,' 'short-attachment') workers could fall back into dependency on the earnings of primary ('stable, long-attachment') workers. For women with poor husbands, there was a subsistence-level, stigmatized form of benefit (McKeen, 1989).

While public pressure forced the Mulroney government to retreat on its initial attempt to de-index Old Age Security pensions, it did put forward a number of proposals and introduce other significant changes to social policy, especially in the areas of child and family benefits and taxation.[5] The strategy for reform was ultimately one of what has been aptly called stealth – restructuring social security programs through technical changes that were announced as part of the federal budget (e.g., partial de-indexing and tax rule changes).[6] These changes were little understood by the public and served to undermine efforts by social policy advocates to mobilize public interest and protest (Battle, 1993: 425). The impact of these reforms was to erode the universality principle and to substantially reduce the rate of increase of federal social expenditures, or as one observer commented, they placed income security benefits on an escalator going down (Gray, 1990; Battle, 1993; Rice and Prince, 1993; Moscovitch, 1990; McBride and Shields, 1993: 66–77).

### Feminism, Family Benefits, and the Politics of Autonomy

The 1980s was another important transition period for the feminist struggle for women's rights and autonomy in social policy. By the early 1980s institutionalized feminism had gained a foothold as a respectable voice on public policy. It had achieved a major success in 1981 with the entrenchment of the women's equality sections in the Charter of Rights and Freedoms. Women's issues were being addressed within the federal state by the various bodies that had been established within the bureaucracy. Funding to women's groups (via the Women's Programme) increased in the early and mid-1980s, and reached a peak in 1987, although cuts would follow (Burt, 1994: 216). At the same time, important changes were beginning to take place within the broader women's movement, and NAC particularly, and these would fully crystallize and transform feminism by the late 1980s and early 1990s. For example, new groups of minority women, especially immigrant and visible minority women, emerged at this time, and there was growing pressure to address questions of racism and to recognize the interrelations of racism, sexism, and classism.[7] Thus, beginning in 1986, NAC's mandate was expanded to incorporate the need to challenge sexist, racist, and classist assumptions. Disabled women also organized and demanded increased attention within the mainstream women's movement.[8] The demands of visible minority and immigrant women and women with disabilities prompted an organizational review of NAC and a major internal debate in 1988 (Burt, 1994: 220; Vickers, et al., 1993: 148). The implementation of the equality clause of the Charter in 1985 also brought a greater focus on equality and legal issues, which increased the activities and profile of legally oriented women's groups such as the Legal Education and Action Fund (LEAF, formed in 1985) and the National Association of Women and the Law (NAWL, formed in 1976). Socialist feminism (and to some extent radical feminism) also began to ascend within NAC, although it would only be towards the end of the decade that this change would fully affect its overall policy orientation and strategies. This voice was strengthened through campaigns against free trade and, increasingly, against the broader restructuring agenda of the Conservative government. Between 1985 and 1988 NAC played a key role in mounting this opposition, involving itself in coalition work with other popular sector groups organized under the Pro-Canada Network. Behind this activity was the recognition that a policy of 'less government,' and the ongoing restructuring of employment (e.g., loss of jobs under free trade), was detrimental to women and their equality rights. While women's participation in the labour force continued to increase in this period, and many secured jobs in management and other professions, most new jobs for women were in low-wage and non-standard (especially part-time) work, and in the sales and service sectors (Armstrong, 1996; Bakker, 1996; Jenson, 1996). Child care, health care, and equal pay legislation were also threatened by the unregulated, privatized economy encouraged under free trade (Bashevkin, 1985: 367). The socialist-feminist and labour-oriented women in and around NAC who formulated its position on free trade (especially members of NAC's subcommittee on employment, such as Marjorie Cohen and Madelaine Parent) urged a shifting of the focus away from traditional 'women's issues' (e.g., day care, abortion, affirmative action, and pay equity) to broader economic and labour issues, such as free trade, privatization, deregulation, and trade policy (Bashevkin, 1985; Vickers et al., 1993: 274; Cohen, 1992). It was not until 1988, however, with funding cuts to women's organizations and the growing challenge instigated by REAL Women and right-wing politicians, that NAC would adopt a full-blown oppositional stance towards the Tory government.

While these important changes were beginning to take place, then, NAC's response to social policy issues in the early and mid-1980s was still very much in the hands of more moderate lobby-oriented feminists who were interested in making changes within the existing system and engaging in debate with the Tories.[9] The issue of women's independent right to benefits continued to be a major theme for this strong contingent through the late 1970s and early 1980s. NAC's pension and family benefits subcommittee, chaired by Louise Dulude, was a centre of this activity, and it was particularly active in the areas of pensions and children's benefits.[10] Pensions took up most of its energies in the early period, with 'pensions for homemakers' becoming a major focus in the early 1980s. Feminists were vocal participants in the 1981 Pensions Conference, and several of them achieved credibility more generally as expert policy analysts (Bob Baldwin, personal interview).[11]

Socialist-minded feminists argued against family-based social policy as a matter of principle, as illustrated, for example, in Margrit Eichler's early 1980s work, but the issue was also consistently brought to the fore by the many challenges to women's independent rights to Unemployment Insurance and Family Allowance benefits in the early 1980s. For example, the Trudeau government proposed that UI entitlement be based on family income (in accordance with a proposal developed by the Economic Council of Canada), and in 1982 it limited the indexing of child benefits to 'six and five' per cent. The value of universality was also questioned at this time, and Finance Minister Marc Lalonde aired the possibility of eliminating the program altogether (Prince, 1984: 99).

National women's organizations (notably NAC and the CACSW) adamantly defended women's right to these benefits, and with much of the focus at this time on family and child benefit programs, they took firm stands on the Family Allowance and the principle of universality. Women's organizations continued to express concern that the gradual transformation of the income security system from a universal emphasis to a selective one would 'force adults to become increasingly dependent on each other within the family' (CACSW, 1982: 3). They recognized that the shift to the family-based Child Tax Credit penalized women with well-off spouses (ibid.). Women's groups claimed that the Family Allowance was 'women's money,' although there continued to be some underlying ambiguity about whether it was *for* women or *for women to give to their children*.[12] In any case, reducing the allowance was seen as an attack on women:

> We have before us three programs for children. There are two going to women and you want to decrease one of those. There is one that goes to the men and there is no rationale behind it [i.e., the child tax exemption] ... The only possible reason that can motivate that kind of thing is that women are not considered as being a political force that is worth thinking about. You can take money away from women whenever you want while if you try even to touch the exemption in any kind of substantial way, the men are going to be screaming and they have far more political clout. (Canada, House of Commons Standing Committee on Health, Welfare and Social Affairs, 1982: (NAC) 51: 33)

Feminists argued that the Family Allowance was at least token recognition of women's work as mothers and an important source of independent income for many women, including those in well-off households: 'The fact is that hundreds, if not thousands, of Canadian women are in that situation [of needing the Allowance] ... So I think this argument ... must be taken seriously' (1982: (NAC) 51: 9). And, 'there is a minority of mothers who do not really need these family allowances. But we are talking about a few fortunate women, as opposed to the average Canadian woman' (1982: (CACSW) 52: 54).

The debate over entitlement intensified with the election of the Mulroney government, with its promotion of the family as the basic unit for social policy and with its right-wing element backing the particular *breadwinner* model of family. The adoption of a targeting emphasis by the government, in which the poor and the truly needy were defined in terms of family units, served only to reinforce the notion of the family as the appropriate unit of support. Proposals were made in relation to several policy areas to increase targeting and adopt family-based entitlement criteria. The Forget Commission recommended that UI be family-income tested – that a two-tiered structure be introduced in which benefits would be based on the number of dependents. The Finance and Economic Affairs Standing Committee also recommended a system of 'joint' taxation in 1986 (Canada, Standing Committee on Finance and Economic Affairs, 1987a). Major women's organizations quickly responded to these proposals with a defence of women's independent entitlement to benefits. With respect to UI, for example, 'We addressed this issue repeatedly in the 1970s as did other organizations concerned with justice and equality ... These concepts were thoroughly discredited as a thinly-veiled attack upon women's income and independence' (NAC, 1986: 32). And, 'the CACSW regards the proposal to base benefits on family income as totally unacceptable. Indeed, we would question whether it would even be legal, given sections 15 and 28 of the Charter' (CACSW, 1986: 23). With respect to the tax system, they argued that 'Too often the focus has been on possible inequities between families, at the expense of equity within the family' (CACSW, 1987a: 5). And, 'NAC supports the individual as the unit of taxation and rejects any system of joint taxation of the spouses because it would greatly jeopardize the financial security of women' (NAC, 1987: 13). Indeed, 'a joint taxation system would have the effect of reducing the individual financial security of married women and we are opposed to its introduction' (CACSW, 1987b: 9).[13]

While feminist commentaries on the Macdonald and Forget commissions' proposals were mainly concerned with the implications for women's jobs, they also voiced strong objections to the family orientation of the envisioned guaranteed annual income plan. The proposal had been that a range of social welfare programs (including the Family Allowance) be replaced with a single, family-income–tested, GAI plan. As feminists argued, 'The major problem ... with all of the proposals for a guaranteed annual income is that all of them are based on family income ... what it does is put them [women] back into a situation of dependency with the family' (Monica Townson, quoted in Dundas, 1987: 7). For 'when family income is the gauge by which social benefits are distributed (and it always is in GAI schemes) the particular needs of women are lost. Women's poverty, except when they are living alone, is hard to see. We talk about poor families, poor kids, poor old people, but the particular poverty of women is invisible when they are in families' (Cohen, 1987: 21).[14]

The debate on the GAI died out in the late 1980s when it became clear that it would not be introduced by government (although, as was later noted by one observer, the 1992 changes to child benefits did in many ways mirror the Macdonald Commission's recommendations; Brigitte Kitchen, personal interview). It is important to note, however, that feminist views on the issue of entitlement did have some influence on the wider progressive social policy community at this time. David Ross, for instance, raised the issue of the unit of entitlement within the Canadian Council on Social Development, with the result that CCSD's proposal for a core income security plan (the central proposal of its 'Work and Income in the Nineties' project) advanced the 'individual' as the basic income accounting unit and recommended that it be phased in gradually as the basic unit for all social security programs.[15] A major consideration in their reasoning was the 'protection of the enhanced economic status and growing economic independence of women' (Ross, 1986: 11). Use of the individual as opposed to the family as the basic unit for the GAI also appealed to these analysts for reasons of technical 'neatness.' Increasing pressure from the political right to preserve the family, especially the male-breadwinner family, however, ultimately prevailed, and some analysts reframed the unit question in ways that eclipsed gender and the issues of independence completely – for example, as a design consideration pertaining to family 'neutrality,' or wanting to ensure that the system did not discourage people from marrying, or create an incentive to form artificial single-parent family units, divorce, or encourage youth to leave home (Van Loon, 1986: 11; Ross, 1986: 14; Wolfson, 1986).

A pivotal moment in the campaign to preserve women's independent entitlement occurred with the mid-1980s' debate over the Family Allowance. The Mulroney government proposed the partial de-indexing of the allowance in 1985 (Bill C-70), stressing in its public justification that inequality would result if 'the wives of bank managers' received the benefit. Women's groups of all ideological bents came together to object to this measure and defend the rights of 'wives' to receive the benefit. Fifty thousand people responded to NAC's call to women to write and send petitions to the prime minister and minister of finance. Quebec groups organized a protest on Parliament Hill, which was attended by a couple of hundred women, and lobbied federal MPs and local politicians. Women's groups from across the country appeared before the Legislative Committee on Bill C-70 and Standing Committee on Health, Welfare, and Social Affairs to oppose the legislation. They included NAC, CACSW, Féderation des femmes du Québec (FFQ),

Coalition pour les allocations familiales (representing eighty Quebec women's groups), Fédération des associations des familles mono-parentales du Québec, Quebec Voice of Women, Réseau d'action et d'information pour les femmes (RAIF), Saskatchewan Action Commit-tee on the Status of Women, and Vancouver Status of Women. The notion at the core of their case was that 'the independent financial security of women must not be eroded ... we are ... categorically op-posed to a reduction in the present benefits of wives on the grounds their husbands have high incomes' (Canada, House of Commons Stand-ing Committee on Health, Welfare and Social Affairs, 1985: (NAC) 9: 9; Canada, Standing Committee on Finance and Economic Affairs, 1987: (NAC) 86: 21).

Several women's groups also argued that the Family Allowance should not be tampered with until there were an equitable sharing of resources within the family.[16] Again, they emphasized that the allowance was an important source of independent income, not just for some, but *all* women: 'In case you say this is an unusual situation [i.e., women not having access to husband's income; women using the family allowance to get out of an abusive relationship], I will remind the committee that for people who are getting married today, the anticipated divorce rate is 40% and rising' (1985: (NAC) 4: 32).

The political opportunity for advancing a strong position on the issue of autonomy and for defending the Family Allowance began to shrink considerably in the mid-1980s, however. A turning point came as femi-nists formulated their response to the Mulroney plan for child benefits. They chose, along with their colleagues and allies within the progres-sive social policy community, to support the Conservative vision for reform of child benefits – a vision that increased the targeting of the system and reinforced family-based eligibility criteria. This choice was made, of course, under the conditions 'not of their own choosing.' But my key point is that influences emanated from *both* macro- and meso-or policy-community levels. For example, shifts in the social and eco-nomic situation of women tended to undermine the argument for women's autonomy and the validity of a gendered perspective on the allowance. Likewise, the increasing participation of women in the labour force reduced the significance this benefit had as a source of indepen-dent income for women and made it especially difficult to mobilize middle-class women. The rhetoric against universality, and the implied message of the Mulroney government and right-wing ideologues that a woman's interests are synonymous with those of her family, may have also contributed to reducing support for the Family Allowance. Louise Dulude – NAC's representative on social policy – was profoundly influenced by her perception that support for the universality of family allowances had declined, even among women.[17] In addition, however, feminists were already heavily invested in the particular messages and strategies of the broader progressive community and milieu created by the more powerful social policy actors. In fact, feminist organizations were now more than ever directly involved with this mainstream and left-liberal sector. It was largely from this vantage point that feminists continued to interpret and represent women's interests on social policy matters, and on family and child benefits reform, which was a major focus at the time. Understanding these additional constraints operating within the policy community context, then, is an important part of the explanation of feminist successes and losses in this field.

### The Moderate Politics of the Social Policy Reform Group

Advocacy organizations that were *not* responsive to the Tory invitation to consult on social policy and/or were not willing to engage within the terms set by the Tories – notably, organized labour – remained for the most part marginal to the debates on social policy. Labour organizations were generally not given a sympathetic ear by the Mulroney government. The Canadian Labour Congress was forced to adopt a defensive position in this period, and it took steps to build alliances with other popular sector groups opposed to the Tory government – for example, becoming involved in the Pro-Canada Network (Smith, 1992). The CLC disagreed from the outset with the parameters of the Tory review of social programs, objecting to the government's unwillingness to dedicate any new money to the social envelope (CLC, 1985; Canada, House of Commons Standing Committee on Health, Welfare and Social Affairs, 1985: (CLC) 9: 55). It was also highly critical of the Tory proposals for family benefits, which were limited to redistributing income *within* the population that had children and only addressed the problem of vertical equity and not other social objectives. The CLC's own approach to poverty was much broader. It entailed increasing the minimum wage, improving UI and Workers' Compensation, setting minimum standards for social assistance, and providing public support for day care. Also overshadowed in this period (although they would achieve a higher profile later) were the voices of newly emerging so-called child poverty groups who were concerned with stemming the tide towards targeting and wanted a public revisiting of the 'universality versus selectivity' question.[18]

Despite fraying relations between the Tory government and the advocacy community, certain organizations did indeed establish a profile as a legitimate voice in the debates. Nationally focused, primarily federally financed, social policy and anti-poverty organizations – with CCSD, NCW, and NAPO at the core – continued to have centre stage in shaping the *progressive* voice on social policy for the mainstream public. CCSD was the largest of these organizations in terms of financial and professional resources and had the capacity for expert social policy analysis. The National Council of Welfare was smaller (a research staff of only two), but with access to government research, it could play an important role in distributing information to other organizations (Haddow, 1990: 27). The reputation of the NCW was also based on the excellence of the work of its director Ken Battle. The National Anti-Poverty Organization also became a more effective body through the 1980s, having had two competent and high-profile directors,[19] although it was still dependent on the expertise and research capacities of other organizations. At the centre of this community was a handful of analysts with 'number-crunching' abilities and an in-depth knowledge of social security and certain tax and transfer programs.[20]

This community continued to follow a left-liberal tradition and, in the role of 'poverty expert,' to legitimize and sustain the poverty concept and anti-poverty cause. The community generated a poverty literature over this period through 'fact books' on poverty and publications on poverty 'lines,' 'estimates,' and 'profiles' (e.g., CCSD, 1983, 1984, 1989; NCW, 1981, 1982, 1983, 1985, 1988).[21] One of the new 'stories' to emerge was the growing disparity between upper- and middle- and lower-income families – that is, upper-income families increased their share of total income at the expense of other families over this period to a value of $2.1 billion (CCSD, 1989: 72). The Canadian Council of Social Development employed the concept of income 'fifths' or 'quintiles' (i.e., the top and bottom ones representing the poorest and richest sectors of society) to convey a message about the unfair distribution of income between the rich and poor. Women's poverty also remained a central focus for anti-poverty proponents (CCSD, 1983, 1984). The discovery of the connection between women and poverty gave way in the early 1980s to the full-blown *feminization of poverty* theme – a term that had emerged earlier within U.S. feminism (it is attributed to Diana Pearce). It became popular in Canada when the media focused on reports produced by CCSD and Statistics Canada (made possible when the latter began to produce a breakout in its poverty publication on single parents). The feminization of poverty ostensibly referred to the rapid increase in the numbers of female single parents and the fact that they formed an increasing proportion of the poor (NCW, 1986b: 7). For example, according to the NCW, only 13.2 per cent of poor families were headed by women in 1961, while their share had climbed to 36.5 per cent by 1985 (1986b: 7). A more critical reading of the data, however, reveals that women's poverty has been characterized by more stability than change (i.e., they represented 56.9 per cent of the poor in 1971 and 60.4 per cent in 1988, and women have always been poor in greater numbers than men). As feminists well knew, and as was increasingly being documented in the growing literature on feminist sociology of the family, it was 'an old problem with a new name' (Harmer, 1992). The latter material shows that poverty (and increasingly, homelessness) is the almost inevitable fate of women living without a man and that the experiences of poverty are compounded for those who are older, non-white, lesbian, or disabled (Harmer, 1992, 1995; and Mandell, 1998). At the root of the problem is the devaluation of women's work both in the home and employment. As Pat Evans and others have suggested, the growing visibility of women's poverty is not the result of any change in objective circumstances but rather, 'its emergence is, in part, socially constructed ... Their poverty is rendered more 'visible' in the absence of a husband, particularly when it leads to the receipt of social assistance benefits' (1991: 174–5). The popular perception created in the early 1980s, nevertheless, was that poverty in Canada 'has the face of a woman' (CCSD, 1984: 22).

If there was a central and defining political activity for the progressive social policy sector at this time, however, it was to provide an 'opposition' to the Tory government. While Mulroney was calling universality 'a sacred trust,' there was great trepidation within these organizations about what the Tory presence would mean for social programs. The perceived intent of the new, majority, right-wing government was to destroy social programs. Indeed, talk of deficit reduction by Finance Minister Wilson in the first mini-budget in November 1984 was something new, and 'struck fear into the hearts of the anti-poverty sector' (Terrance Hunsley, personal interview).

The directors of the three core national social policy organizations, who shared a history of working together (for instance, during the 1970s social security review and the great pension debate) reacted to these events by forming a small coalition group, the Social Policy Reform Group (SPRG), whose purpose was to present a unified front and to ensure that they would continue to have a voice on social policy. They agreed that they would also participate in the debates as separate organizations and to pursue projects and mandates independently (for instance, CCSD's Work and Income in the Nineties (WIN) campaign was an important contribution to the GAI discussion; CCSD, 1986a, 1986b, 1987). Women's organizations were perceived as obvious and useful allies, and a conscious decision was made to invite some women's groups to participate within SPRG. NAC and the CACSW were brought into the alliance, as were the Canadian Association of Social Workers, and later in the 1980s, the National Pensioners and Senior Citizens Federation. A decision was also evidently made *not* to invite organized labour. According to Bob Baldwin, director of social policy for the CLC, some SPRG members had a general concern that the two organizations would not be able to come together on strategy questions. A more specific issue at the time might well have been that the CLC and NAC took opposite sides on the issue of homemakers' pensions, and NAC's representative was concerned that clashes on this within SPRG would undermine any chance of this reform being adopted (Bob Baldwin, personal interview).[22]

SPRG was very successful in capturing the spotlight on social policy issues in the mid- to late 1980s (disbanding in 1989). Through press releases and at parliamentary hearings it remained an outspoken critic on the numerous substantive proposals on social policy put forward by the government and federal commissions. It was consistently represented within the media as leading the opposition on social policy matters (there were, in fact, few opposition MPs at this time). As one SPRG member observed, 'we were perceived to be much more powerful than we really were ... we were a bit of a paper tiger' (Patrick Johnston, personal interview). With its credibility, SPRG was regularly invited to meet with Minister of Finance Michael Wilson and other cabinet ministers as part of the pre-budget consultation process. SPRG also had a mobilizing effect on the broader voluntary community in Ottawa, which included, for instance, the Vanier Institute of the Family, the Canadian Institute of Child Health, the Child Daycare Advocacy Association, and teachers' associations. It was effective in building solidarity around its positions, and at the same time it created a space for these organizations to become informed and to participate in the debates. The 'last Wednesday of the month club,' a venue that was organized and attended by

SPRG members, provided an opportunity for other organizations to share their concerns and develop an understanding of current issues,[23] while certain SPRG organizations were able to tutor groups on the complex intricacies of the tax transfer system and its progressive solutions (Robert Glossop, personal interview).

Examining SPRG's positions more critically, it is clear that theirs was largely a defensive response to the Tories, born out of fear of what might happen rather than of a strong positive philosophy or goal. SPRG member organizations saw their role as trying, perhaps, to 'slow down, but not substantially alter, the course of the Tory beast' (Terrance Hunsley, personal interview). SPRG members had low expectations of what could be achieved under the right-wing government, especially in the context of economic recession – as indicated, for example, in the following responses by SPRG representatives to NDP MP Margaret Mitchell's questioning during hearings on child benefits:

> Certainly one could hope for an increase in child benefits. There is nothing that we have said that would preclude that. It is just that, given the economic climate we are in now, we see the symmetry of redirecting resources from a regressive benefit to a progressive benefit as a feasible approach. I guess it is just a matter of judgement. I mean, it has taken so long to get this far, we would not want to see, frankly, the government say we are not getting enough support for this, so we will not bother trying it. (Canada, House of Commons Standing Committee on Health, Welfare and Social Affairs, 1985: (NCW) 9: 32)

> I would like to say very specifically the way in which we see the situation now. It is not that we are content with half a loaf. The situation is that we are given a choice between a half-loaf and no loaf at all. And in that situation, given the parameters that exist right now, we will take the half-loaf. (Ibid., 1985: (SPRG) 9: 42)

> It is the broad direction about which we have a sense where we are moving. It is the first time in years that we have had any sense of even moving in that direction, which is why I think we are trying to encourage and support continuing to move. It is not the end. (Ibid., 1985: (NAPO) 9: 43)

SPRG member groups were committed to formulating a 'minimum program' – something they could all agree to: 'The positions that are presented ... are the positions that we all agree on. It does not mean we do not agree on the other points, but they are the positions that we consider to be minimum, a minimum program, which is the priority of all the participating groups' (ibid., 1985: (SPRG) 9: 39).

The subject of child and family benefits was a central focus of debate through the mid-1980s. Some social policy advocates had since the 1970s called for improvements to child benefits, especially the Child Tax Credit, which they saw as a precursor to a more comprehensive guaranteed annual income (negative income tax type) program. This debate was reopened in January 1985 with the minister of health and welfare's consultation paper on 'child and elderly benefits.' SPRG's official stand was to endorse the direction and fiscal parameters of Tory proposals, especially their child benefit proposal, which they saw as a major step towards a more progressive system and the best that could be expected from a government that prioritized deficit reduction and private sector growth (ibid., 1985: (NCW) 21/3/85, 9: 31; SPRG, 1985a; NCW, 1985; NAPO, 1985). Its approach was clearly at odds with that taken by the labour community, notably, the Canadian Labour Congress. The CLC had three primary objections to SPRG's (and especially CCSD's) approach: the CLC saw social policy organizations as, first, shying away from attributing difficulties in the labour market to government policy; second, as failing to challenge the federal government on the need for spending restraint in the social policy area; and, third, as adopting a position that ultimately supported the reconstruction of social programs as more targeted (Bob Baldwin, personal interview). Divisions between these groups would intensify again when the CLC objected to CCSD's 1988 proposal for a core guaranteed income program, a plan that assumed conditions of high unemployment and a labour market divided into peripheral and core workers.[24] Such clashes were felt as well by the wider political left community. Not long after SPRG was formed, the Canadian Conference of Catholic Bishops convened a meeting in Ottawa to discuss social policy issues; it was attended by representatives of a number of labour and other groups active on social policy. This gathering was, in significant measure, a reaction against the approach that SPRG had adopted. SPRG was perceived by the organizers as having high-profile progressive spokespeople, but many felt it had conceded far too much to the Tories and the drift to the political right (Bob Baldwin, personal interview). Following this meeting, a group came together to produce a declaration ('A Time to Stand Together ... A Time for Social Solidarity'), which set forth an alternative political agenda (Bleyer, 1992), and many who participated subsequently became involved in the Canadian Centre for Policy Alternatives, the Pro-Canada Network, and the Council of Canadians, for which the issues of free trade and employment took centre stage.

In retrospect, this period marked a significant narrowing in the outlook of the mainstream and left-liberal social policy community. While progressive organizations had always sought a more redistributive system, that goal was given quite a specific and moderate interpretation under SPRG's leadership: 'targeting' would mean eliminating tax benefits for the rich, and there would be no *further* spending cuts to the income support system.[25] The consuming goal of SPRG organizations, in particular, CCSD, NCW, and NAPO, was one of convincing the government to address tax exemptions (e.g., the child tax exemption and the spousal exemption) that disproportionately benefited the rich, either by eliminating them or converting them to credits. This issue, and that of maintaining the funding level for social programs, were the main ones up for discussion with the minister of finance (e.g., NCW, 1985; Canada, House of Commons Legislative Committee on Bill C-70, 1985: (NCW) 4: 18; (CCSD) 4: 3; (NAPO) 3: 14; Canada, House of Commons Standing Committee on Health, Welfare and Social Affairs, 1985: (NCW) 9: 27; (NAPO) 9: 17; (CCSD) 10: 4). In keeping with this framework, the key criteria for judging any policy or program became its ability to contribute to 'vertical equity' (i.e., the 'bottom-line' of who wins and who loses with respect to disposable income), and this was increasingly the focus of SPRG's analysis and critique (e.g., SPRG, 1985b; 1985c; 1986; NCW, 1986a). The only real areas of dispute between SPRG organizations and the Department of Finance was where to draw the line as between the 'winners' and the 'losers' (i.e., whether to include the middle class among the winners) and how high to set the level of benefits – social policy groups argued that people with 'moderate' incomes should be included under the program, while the federal government tended to want to target lower down the income scale. CCSD's main criticism of the Macdonald Commission's recommended guaranteed annual income plan, for example, was that it was not generous enough and that it left most people only marginally better off and still below the poverty line (e.g., Ross, 1986a; 1986b). The main areas of contention were, indeed, technicalities – threshold levels, tax-back rates, and turning points – with progressive analysts putting their energies into 'out-modelling' the Finance Department in the building of a more targeted and acceptable Child Tax Credit system – ideally, one that assigned more money below the low income threshold level, but stayed within the existing budget.[26]

## The Further Derailing of Feminist Ideals

A conjunctural moment in the closure of a feminist politics of autonomy occurred when representatives of the women's movement within SPRG (NAC and CACSW) chose, with their social policy colleagues, to endorse the family-based Child Tax Credit as the primary mechanism for family income support. The Family Allowance was thus assigned a marginal place in the child benefits system (specifically, they advocated eliminating the Child Tax Exemption, increasing the Child Tax Credit, and maintaining the Family Allowance). Feminist participants acknowledged that this was not the ideal solution from the standpoint of women's groups (who wanted the allowance increased), yet they had come to accept that such a demand was unrealistic given the fiscal concerns of the federal government: 'The feelings of some of the members of the group [SPRG] are that we would, as mentioned earlier, like an increase in the family allowance but that, given the very restrictive framework of keeping the same amount of money – we are not getting any new money in – and the situation, which is that very low income families right now are in a very bad position ... it seemed to all of us in this group that the priority should be, when this money is taken out of the exemption, to give it to poor people, because at this point their need is so obvious and crying, they are the ones who should have first call on it' (Canada, House of Commons Standing Committee on Health, Welfare, and Social Affairs, 1985: (SPRG) 9: 46).

This choice was powerfully conditioned, however, by the policy agenda of feminism's more powerful allies within the social policy community. The mainstream progressive cause, as defined primarily by the 'big three' (largely male) organizations of CCSD, NCW, and NAPO, prioritized vertical equity and the 'bottom-line' question of the benefit level for the poor at the direct expense of the principles of universality and horizontal equity – principles that had traditionally had purchase within the community. SPRG rejected the Child Tax Exemption, for example, because of its negative impact on vertical equity and disregarded its contribution to horizontal equity (its equalizing effect on the disposable incomes of those with and those without children – one reason why the CLC supported this measure; Canadian Labour Congress, 1985; Canada, Standing Committee on Health, Welfare and Social Affairs, 1985: (CLC) 9: 55). While several SPRG members may still have privately supported the concept of universality, some high-profile analysts thought it had become a 'red flag' that diverted discussion away from the more urgent and substantive issues of ensuring adequate income for the poor and addressing the income gap between the rich and the poor (CCSD, 1985b). According to one observer, for instance, the issue of 'universality versus selectivity' had become cast in somewhat black and white terms: those who favoured universality were labelled and dismissed in the media as 'bleeding-heart' leftists or communists, while those who favoured selectivity were cast as the new modern business-minded breed of the future (David Ross, personal interview). There was an attempt by some, therefore, to avoid the *language* of universality by arguing, for instance, that the distinction between universal and selective instruments was a false one since they could be designed to have the same net effect with respect to distribution (Ross, 1985; CCSD, 1986a). Some began to frame the preferred goal as 'universal access' to an adequate standard of living (CCSD, 1985b: 1). The Family Allowance had become within these terms just one of several child benefit programs (merely part of the 'child benefits system'), the goal of which was to be *redistribution*. Such an understanding left little space for feminists or any other group to defend the Family Allowance as a distinct program and as having a unique impact and implications.

Dynamics *within* SPRG came into play as well. Feminists in this context were forced to compromise in a negotiating situation in which they had relatively less power and wherein the onus was on achieving a *minimum* program on which all could agree. Notwithstanding the personal influence of the individuals participating within SPRG, women's groups were more marginal actors vis-à-vis the core group of social policy organizations, and poverty and the design of social security programs were for them more peripheral concerns. Moreover, income security issues were fading in importance within the institutional women's movement given the new urgency, especially for left feminists, of the issues of free trade and women's declining employment.

Women's groups were also set apart from the inner group of analysts within SPRG because of having fewer resources to dedicate to social policy analysis and producing hard data. The CACSW, in particular, viewed participation within SPRG as a low priority – certainly, the council's mid-1980s president did not count social policy and poverty issues as among the 'women's issues' for which the council was responsible.[27] By then, the council had become well populated with Tory partisans who lacked interest in social policy (Burt, 1998). Feminists also encountered resistance from within SPRG on the specific issue of the best unit for entitlement. For example, it would appear that certain SPRG participants were not particularly receptive to feminist arguments about women's autonomy (Louise Dulude, personal interview). Feminists had little real choice under these conditions but to sacrifice their long-time stake in the Family Allowance program and to agree to give full support to the vertical equity cause. The decision marked a withdrawal by the women's movement from the goal of individualization for this area of policy and a failure to adequately represent the strength of feeling many women's groups had concerning the Family Allowance (given that, many, if not most women's groups, including the CACSW (1984), had been calling for increases to the allowance).

A period of intense struggle over universality and women's rights to independent treatment came to an end, then, with feminists choosing to set aside long-term equity and autonomy concerns for the sake of more immediate gains for the poor. On the one hand, these ideas lost credibility in the face of rising poverty rates for single mothers and a growing opposition to universality. On the other hand, however, the defensive politics of the more powerful social policy and anti-poverty organizations, narrowly cast in terms of redistribution and vertical equity, played an important part in closing political space for such claims and for defending the Family Allowance program. While joining the Social Policy Reform Group was a pragmatic move for the institutionalized women's movement in the face of the Tory onslaught against social policy, it was a collaboration that ultimately, if unwittingly, helped facilitate the neo-liberal movement towards a more targeted, poverty-oriented, and familialist, social policy system.

In retrospect, this period marked the heyday of feminist involvement in the world of moderate, mainstream social policy politics. Indeed, the institutionalized movement's status as a legitimate player in the debate on child benefits quickly deteriorated from this point onwards, as did gender as a variable of discussion in the field. As I argue in the next chapter, however, these changes were the result of processes that were more subtle and complex, and they involved a wider range of political actors, than is often implied by use of the term *neo-liberalism*.

# Feminism and Child Poverty Discourse in the Late 1980s to Mid-1990s: 'Writing Women Out'

The late 1980s to mid-1990s witnessed a further closure of a feminist politics of autonomy in social policy. Indeed, at this time feminists seemed to abandon altogether the more mainstream causes of promoting income security and targeting the poor. While broad social forces clearly drove feminists towards a more oppositional stance vis-à-vis the emerging neo-liberal agenda – an agenda that was truly destructive to women – the argument presented here is that they were also in many ways *forced to take their leave* of the debate on social policy, especially the child benefits debate. One can certainly trace these changes to the undermining effects that the funding cuts to women's organizations had, as well as to the emergence of a new sweeping political ideology that individualized social problems and defined poor women as undeserving. Yet, we should not overlook the ways that feminist activities continued to be directly constrained by the political and discursive strategies of the left-liberal sector of the social policy community. I argue that the project of this sector to rework and refocus the topic of poverty to highlight the issue of so-called child poverty (an issue that was also taken up by neo-liberal governments) played into a process that undermined feminist credibility in social policy debates and in many ways facilitated the move towards a new gender-blind approach to social policy.

In a context of the new global economy, which featured increased mobility of capital, globalization of production, and interdependence among nations, the Canadian economy continued to decline. There was an economic recession beginning in the late 1980s (peaking in 1990–1) which was followed by a period of 'jobless growth.' The level of government debt and deficit tripled between the early 1980s and early

1990s (Liberal Party of Canada, 1993: 19), and the unemployment rate settled at a new average high (10.3 per cent in 1993, 18 per cent for youth; Canada, Human Resources Development, 1994: 17). The restructuring of employment continued to move towards a two-tier pattern in which some 'good' jobs were created (i.e., full-time, skilled, well paid, and unionized) at the same time as there was a large expansion of 'bad' jobs (i.e., minimum wage, low skill, and non-standard). Family incomes fell dramatically, record numbers of families were pushed into poverty, the average family was left worse off than it was in 1980 (Brodie, 1995: 74), and increasing numbers of people turned to social assistance – three million Canadians in March 1993 (Canada, Human Resources Development, 1994: 19).

Economic policy underwent critical shifts beginning with the second mandate of the Mulroney government in the late 1980s and continuing through the early years of the Chrétien government. The re-election of the Conservatives in 1988 prompted a more open turn to a neo-liberal policy agenda. The Tories seized on the theme of competitiveness to provide a rationale for a program of reducing the deficit, controlling inflation rates, cutting social programs, expanding training and labour force programs, downsizing, and enhancing productivity within the public sector (Phillips, 1994a). The priority of the Conservatives' 1992 budget, for instance, was to promote greater reliance on the private sector and market forces, followed by deficit reduction, inflation control, free trade, and developing a new consensus about the role of government (Brodie, 1994: 17–18). While the Liberals, elected in 1993, promised to balance the goal of deficit reduction with the goals of economic growth, employment, and human welfare (Liberal Party of Canada, 1993), they ultimately adopted much the same neo-liberal paradigm.[1] For example, they ratified the North American Free Trade Agreement (without negotiating the side agreements as promised) and, in their first two budgets, prioritized deficit reduction over employment and infrastructure development and attacked social welfare programs and the system of federal–provincial cost-sharing that funded them (Brodie, 1995).

The radicalization of the broader political sphere, which had begun in the mid-1980s, held course into the 1990s with popular sector groups mobilizing under the Pro-Canada Network (refounded as Action Canada Network in 1991) and playing a major and visible role in opposing Tory proposals. Focal points for this opposition included the goods and services tax (GST), the 1988 election, the implementation of the free trade agreement, and the Meech Lake and Charlottetown debates. Women's groups, and NAC in particular, were es ful in opposing the Conservative government during the debates, challenging both the agreement and the exclusionary, elite-driven negotiating process (Burt, 1994: 221; Bashevkin, 1996). The failure of the Charlottetown Accord went some way in discrediting the Tory method of governing by elites and was a major success for the popular sector and women's movement.

Not surprisingly, perhaps, a new climate of strained relations appeared between the federal state and the voices of the broader political community. The Conservatives embarked on a full-scale attack on the legitimacy and credibility of advocacy groups, labelling them 'special interests' and therefore not representative of 'real' or 'ordinary' Canadians (Jenson and Phillips, 1996: 124; Brodie, 1995: 69). The federal budgets of 1989, 1990, and 1991[2] announced increasingly larger cuts to interest group funding. There were two other aspects to this backlash, as Jane Jenson and Susan Phillips argue. First, public consultations began in 1990 to give greater weight to the voices of individuals, as opposed to groups (1996: 126). Second, centres within the federal bureaucracy that represented certain categories of citizens were shut down. For example, the Tories cancelled or dispersed programs operating within the Department of Secretary of State, and closed the department itself in 1993 (Jenson and Phillips, 1996: 120). Urged on by the anti-feminist wing (i.e., the Tory 'family caucus') and REAL women, the Tories made significant cuts to the funding of women's groups[3] – a move that was perceived by many as retribution for their stance on the Charlottetown Accord. The Tories also refused after 1988 to participate in NAC's annual lobby of politicians. While the Liberals initially seemed to promise a greater openness to consultation and democratic process, they effectively continued and even stepped up their funding cuts and ideological attacks on the credibility of certain interest groups.[4] They also proceeded to eliminate bodies within the federal state that represented societal interests, the most blatant move being the 1995 elimination of the 'women's state' (i.e., the CACSW and Women's Programme; Jenson and Phillips, 1996). Thus, while the Action Canada Network and other oppositional coalitions have continued to fight the Liberal government's neo-liberal proposals, economic recession, repeated funding reductions, and efforts to marginalize these groups have severely weakened their influence within the universe of political discourse.

**The Imprint of Neo-liberalism on Social Policy**

The Tories adopted a more decisive approach to social policy in their second mandate – attacking both social programs and the idea of poverty itself. For example, in the early 1990s, right-wing ideologues tried to establish an *absolute* definition of poverty in place of the standard view that poverty is a *relative* concept (Sarlo, 1992). The absolute model was taken up by the Senate Sub-committee on Poverty (chaired by Barbara Greene), which argued that poverty was not a serious problem in Canada (Senate, Standing Committee on Health and Welfare, Social Affairs, Seniors and the Status of Women, Sub-committee on Poverty, 1993).[5] The Conservatives proceeded to reduce social spending, dismantle universal rights, and shift responsibility for programs to the provinces (e.g., via the failed Meech Lake Accord). In a series of budget measures between 1986 and 1991, they withdrew massive amounts of funding from social programs, cutting the Established Program Financing (EPF) plan and the Canada Assistance Programme (i.e., the federal transfers to the provinces for social assistance and social services, health care, and post-secondary education), and making deep cuts to Unemployment Insurance[6] by withdrawing the federal contribution to the program and reducing eligibility and benefit levels. They also eliminated universality from Old Age Security (the 1989 'clawback') and child benefits systems (first clawing back the Family Allowance, and then eliminating it altogether). By de-indexing child benefits, the gradual erosion of these benefits was ensured, while other changes effectively eroded progressivity within the tax system (Battle and Torjman, 1995; Rice and Prince, 1993).

The Liberal approach to social policy reform was more complex than that of the Conservatives, at least initially. Their social security review process entailed extensive consultation with the public, through hearings held across the country.[7] Advocacy groups were provided with funding to allow them to make presentations, although as Jenson and Phillips point out, the review was careful about giving undue attention to groups (rather than individuals).[8] These initiatives suggested a greater focus on social policy and a return to a social-liberal doctrine. Indeed, evident in the Axworthy discussion paper were notions of equal opportunity, of a safety net that did not stigmatize, and of redistribution (the guaranteed annual income was one of the options advanced). A closer analysis of this document, however, reveals that this was social-liberalism with a difference. The Liberals favoured a strong targeting orientation and viewed the role of the social welfare system as providing a safety net for those who fail to find their niche in the market economy, rather than as protecting against the failure of the market (Maioni, 1994). Following on the approach adopted by the Macdonald Commission, and earlier by the Tories, with respect to training and UI, and by the Organization for Economic Cooperation and Development (OECD) and the Economic Council of Canada (ECC, 1992), the discussion paper advocated active rather than passive measures and preferred the metaphor of the trampoline or springboard (bouncing people back into the labour market) to that of the safety net (Canada, HRDC, 1994: 25).[9] The Liberal government wanted to alter social welfare to place emphasis on employability, adaptability, and self-reliance and to remove disincentives to work through 'active measures' such as counseling, training, and relocation: 'Our aspiration is to build a social security system that enables all Canadians ... to exploit their talents, lead fulfilling lives, and experience the dignity of work' (ibid.).

Government support would be targeted only to those who 'demonstrate a willingness and commitment to self-help' (ibid.). This approach was antithetical to the concept of universal citizenship rights. It implicitly distinguished the deserving from the undeserving, between the competent or 'good' citizens who achieve self-reliance (by getting and keeping a job, or being adaptable enough to acquire skills and move into new jobs as the demand changes) and the incompetent or 'bad' citizens who 'have difficulty' and are 'dependent' on social benefits (Brodie, 1994: 57; 1995: 61). Under the UI system, for example, lower benefits would be provided to 'frequent' as opposed to 'occasional' claimants. At the same time, individuals were held to blame for their own poverty. It was incumbent upon them to reduce their risk of poverty by making better personal decisions such as 'staying in school,' 'delaying child bearing,' or 'avoiding marriage breakdown' – ideas that were first articulated in the early 1990s by the Macdonald Commission report and Economic Council of Canada: 'Society as a whole should ... put more effort into encouraging the kinds of individual decisions that will lead to personal success' (ECC, 1992: 55).

People should also save for 'a rainy day' so that when they do 'experience earnings difficulties' they can 'utilize those savings' (ibid., 1992: 57). The poor were portrayed as a burden on the public purse and society and as an underclass on the margins of society:

Only a small proportion of the population is truly destitute and has no opportunity for achieving some level of self-sufficiency. (ibid., 1992: 18)

Unemployment and the associated poverty are not equally distributed ... Two out of three Canadians will never be poor in their working lives. For the other third, however, spells of joblessness and poverty are a reality. Within this group, there is a growing segment that is poor and/or unemployed for prolonged periods. (ibid., 1992: 54)

The social security review was ultimately pre-empted by the minister of finance, whose 1995 budget firmly directed Liberal social policy back onto a neo-liberal track. Guided by its fiscal agenda, the Liberal government pursued a course of restructuring and reprivatization, limiting its 'fiscal exposure' by targeting benefits to only the most needy, cutting or eliminating them for middle-income people, and shifting more of the cost of social welfare to the provinces, to municipalities, and to families – the latter of whom were increasingly expected to take on roles as consumers in the marketplace. They made major cuts to transfer payments to the provinces for health, post-secondary education, and social assistance; established a new funding mechanism (the Canada Health and Social Transfer) which gave less money but more responsibility and flexibility to the provinces for the delivery of these services and programs; and made huge cuts to public sector jobs and the UI program (Battle and Torjman, 1995; Cohen, 1997).[10] Child benefit programs were the one policy area left open for possible enhancement, although governments wanted tight fiscal limitations on any new initiative and assumed the goal of greater targeting. The idea of 'taking children off of welfare' took hold and became a focal point for federal and provincial discussion in 1996–7. New policy measures would follow in the late 1990s, the most significant being a new National Child Benefit program in 1998 and federal–provincial–territorial agreement in 1999 on a National Children's Agenda, and as part of this, an Early Childhood Development Initiative.

**Feminist Politics: A Radical Turn**

An important change in the social policy orientation of the women's movement took place in the late 1980s and early 1990s. This change marked the beginning of the end of its participation in mainstream social policy debate, with its focus on targeted programs and family poverty. Understanding this change in outlook requires attending to more activities and processes than one might expect, however. NAC's interest and involvement dissolved quickly following its departure from the Social Policy Reform Group (SPRG) in the late 1980s,[11] although this event was itself a reflection of broader changes taking place both in and outside the women's movement. It is not surprising perhaps that certain policy struggles would fall off the feminist agenda, given the level of funding crises experienced by women's organizations. By 1995, for example, only 27 per cent of NAC's annual budget came from federal sources, down from nearly 90 per cent during the early 1980s. Operating under its highest deficit since inception,[12] NAC became much more reliant on volunteer efforts, and its ability to intervene in policy debates was affected severely.

A number of other important factors also weighed in on the situation, however. First, and most obviously, the institutionalized women's movement *lost interest* in income security measures as a strategy for advancing women's equality. The changes that had begun to take place within the women's movement, and in NAC in particular, in the mid-1980s were in full evidence by the late 1980s and early 1990s. According to Sylvia Bashevkin, feminist activists generally were divided, especially during the years after 1988, between militants who saw little reason to cooperate with the Conservatives and pragmatists who were concerned about the consequences of further polarization of the movement away from the government (1996: 236). By the 1990s, however, NAC had largely become a more diverse, broadly focused, and left-wing political force. Marginalized women had achieved a greater voice within NAC. For example, by 1991 NAC had one-fifth of its executive positions reserved for women from disabled, Aboriginal, or visible minority backgrounds (Bashevkin, 1996: 222). All of this had led to a greater sensitivity and movement to a politics of diversity and inclusion, especially by the time of the 1992 constitutional debate (Findlay, 1998). Socialist feminists and labour and union-oriented women had also by then become dominant within NAC's leadership, a turning point being the election of Lynn Kaye as president in 1988 (*Studies in Political Economy*, 1994: 57). Changes in NAC's leadership and direction meant, among other things, that some NAC members who had been involved previously in social policy and income support issues withdrew their participation. NAC also established closer connections to union and working-class women and to labour organizations through its participation in the Action Canada Network and other coalitions opposing free trade and the Meech Lake and Charlottetown accords (*Studies in Political Economy*, 1994). For example, NAC now had a closer relationship with the Canadian Labour Congress, and this involved working together on an ad hoc basis. Thus, factors such as expanded interests and labour connections, the greater influence of union women within NAC (particularly at the level of its committees and executive), as well as women's deteriorating employment situation generally (predominating in the 'bad job' sector and part-time employment, and their growing vulnerability because of changes to UI), all contributed to a conviction within the women's movement that more could be gained by focusing on employment-oriented strategies (to improve employment opportunities, pay, and child care, and so on). Many 'working' and union women viewed income security programs with ambivalence. Such benefits did not fit easily with their broader demand for equality in employment, and some viewed it as a form of wage supplementation that benefited only a select group of women (i.e., women at home; Barbara Cameron, Christa Freiler, personal interviews).[13] This outlook was reinforced by the fact that the Family Allowance payment had diminished substantially as a source of independent income for women as a group, owing to the increased proportion of women in the paid labour force and the decline of its value as the result of changes made in the mid-1980s by the Tories (the partial de-indexing of the benefit in 1985 and the 1989 introduction of a clawback).

At the same time, the mainstream debate on child benefits began to appear to feminists as a relatively narrow and limited concern, given the new and large threat that neo-liberal policy posed for the safety net as a whole. Feminists were concerned about the detrimental impact that the dismantling of social programs and loss of national standards would have on women. Reduced social services meant a greater burden of care work for women – something that would further undermine women's employment participation and prospects for equality, not to mention increasing their personal daily toil. The downloading of responsibility for social policy to the provinces would, likewise, allow provincial governments (equally obsessed with reducing their deficits) to reform social assistance in ways that, again, seriously affect women, especially single mothers.

Second, quite possibly there was a perception among feminists that other progressive actors were already representing women's interests in the debates on income support. For example, the newly formed child poverty organizations were a credible and respected voice in the debates on child benefits, and although women's groups objected strongly to the focus on *child* poverty (as I will discuss below), these organizations were nevertheless broadly perceived as allies in the political context of the late 1980s. They sought many of the same goals as women's organizations, and their proposals for the reform of child benefits would go some distance in addressing the poverty of single mothers.

Another important aspect of these processes – among the aspects that have generally been obscured until now – had to do with the way that the discursive conditions of the period effectively denied feminists a meaningful presence in the mainstream debate on social policy. First, the basis of women's claims-making in the terrain of poverty policy was clearly undermined by the neo-liberal constructions referred to earlier, namely, the distinction between 'good,' self-reliant, citizens and 'bad,' dependent, or needy citizens, wherein women and single mothers disproportionately fell (Brodie, 1996a: Evans, 1996). Women were cast in this discourse as workers, like men. The problem with respect to single mothers, for example, according to the Axworthy review, was to get them off welfare and into the labour market. They were expected to achieve 'self-reliance' and to 'leap successfully from social assistance to the independence of a job' (even a low-paying one), and if they did not do this they risked passing on to their children 'a cycle of low achievement and joblessness' (Canada, Human Resources Development, 1994: 47, 70).[14] As I discuss further below, however, there was little recognition in this perspective of the extra societal barriers facing single mothers in their quest for self-reliance (Brodie, 1996a; Evans, 1996), and apart from these references to single mothers, women had little visibility in the discourse generated by the Axworthy review (Evans, 1997).

Second, and perhaps less recognized, however, the feminist voice was undermined by the strategic (discursive) choices taken by feminists' more powerful allies, left-liberal social policy organizations, participating in national social policy and poverty debates. The latter organizations altered the discursive terrain in a significant way, namely, by framing and promoting the theme of child poverty. As I argue below, their 1990s' reframing of the poverty problem around this theme had serious, if unintended, consequences for feminist agency in the national discussion of poverty and child benefits – in effect, contributing to writing women out of the poverty problem and undermining feminist credibility in this set of debates.

## The Progressive Social Policy Community and the Child Poverty Debate

While relations between progressive and government actors were marked by coolness and even hostility in this period, the full force of this treatment was reserved for the 'popular sector' – groups organized under the Action Canada Network, including the CLC and NAC, who were involved in a broad strategy of opposing the federal government's economic and constitutional proposals. These proposals, as already described, aimed to eliminate federal responsibility for social policy, dismantle national standards for social programs, restructure employment, and threaten jobs. The opposition to these proposals tended to be labelled as radicals and 'special interest' groups, and they were almost completely marginal to the 'mainstream' sector of national social policy and anti-poverty organizations and the debate on income security programs. Indeed, differences between the CLC and the left-liberal sector, which began with the election of the Mulroney government, crystallized further in the late 1980s.

It was a somewhat different story for the national left-liberal sector, making up organizations primarily interested in influencing the reform of income support and child benefits programs. These organizations were, in contrast, able to retain their collective reputation as the voice of progressives on social policy and poverty, although they also clearly suffered from significant cuts and reconfigurations, and there were certainly important differences between them in terms of their ability to gain the government's ear. For example, the Canadian Council for Children and Youth was eliminated, and the Canadian Council on Social Development lost its sustaining grant as of the end of the 1992–3 fiscal year and had to scramble for research contracts in order to survive.[15] The National Council of Welfare continued to function but receded into the background somewhat following the resignation of its high-profile director Ken Battle. On the other hand, the Maytree Foundation established the Caledon Institute of Social Policy, which is a small, ostensibly non-partisan, social policy 'think tank' headed by Battle, and this organization became a prominent player in social welfare debates. Indeed, Battle was willing to work closely with and for the federal Liberals; for example, he designed the proposed Seniors Benefit and new Child Tax Credit, and he went on to be a consultant to federal human resources ministers in late 1996 and early 1997 (Dobrowolsky and Saint-Martin, 2002). In the mid-1990s the

National Anti-Poverty Organization, led by Lynn Toupin, was evidently one of the few long-time social policy organizations that managed to retain its federal funding.[16] While the Social Policy Reform Group had disbanded in the late 1980s (viewed by its members as no longer serving a purpose),[17] new anti-poverty advocacy groups came into greater prominence from the early 1990s onwards, namely, child poverty groups such as the Child Poverty Action Group (CPAG) and Campaign 2000. CPAG was primarily concerned with the increasing poverty of families with children, and its platform emphasized prevention and the principles of universality, horizontal equity, and social responsibility for children. By the mid-1990s CPAG had become a self-confident 'spokes-group' on poverty with a fully articulated vision and agenda for the reform of social security,[18] and it was among the few social policy organizations with credibility within federal circles. CPAG was given funding from Human Resources Development Canada, for example, to develop options for a reformed child benefits system.

'Child poverty' became the major banner in this period under which the left-liberal sector mobilized, and child poverty groups played a primary role in organizing the campaign. While this issue had a material reality (indeed, child poverty in Canada grew from 15.1 per cent of children in 1981 to 18.2 per cent in 1991; CCSD, 1994: 122),[19] the theme was adopted primarily for its potential to give poverty a 'human face' and thereby win public support for preserving, possibly expanding, social programs. It provided grounds for these groups to intervene in debates on child benefits, wherein they made a strong bid, at least initially,[20] to retain the Family Allowance Programme. CPAG and its allies, for example, viewed the reductions to (and clawback of) this program as a significant withdrawal of federal support from mainstream, middle- and modest-income families (e.g., Canada, Senate, Standing Committee on Social Affairs, Science and Technology, 1989–90: (CPAG) 21: 40; (Group of Seven) 20: 21). Likewise, they strongly opposed the introduction of the Child Tax Benefit Programme because they saw it as 'putting a nail in the coffin of universality,' a serious abrogation of the principle of horizontal equity, and a withdrawal of commitment to children and parents and to social responsibility for childraising (e.g., Canada, House of Commons Legislative Committee on Bill C-80, 1991–2: (CPAG/SPCMT) 5: 27; (Vanier Institute), 6: 76; Canada, Senate, Standing Committee on Social Affairs, Science and Technology, 1989–90: (Vanier Institute) 21: 65).

In the late 1980s CPAG organized a network of social policy groups willing to focus on and advance the theme of child poverty. A 'Group of Seven' social policy organizations formed for the purposes of public education and lobbying on the issue of child poverty.[21] The CCSD subsequently became involved in researching and publishing Campaign 2000's annual report card on child poverty, and this subject became a regular feature of mainstream poverty reports such as the CCSD's 1989 and 1994 fact books. These mobilizing efforts continued into the 1990s under Campaign 2000, a group established by CPAG in 1991 (and funded by the Laidlaw Foundation) with a goal of building a national coalition to keep child poverty in the public eye and to pressure the federal government to follow through on a 1989 pledge to end child poverty.[22] Not all social policy groups were initially willing to join this bandwagon. For example, NAPO initially believed that the focus on children would place categories of poor in competition with each other. Some were unhappy with the family-centred orientation of the child poverty focus, while others, such as the Caledon Institute, did not agree with the emphasis on universality.[23] There was even some tension within CPAG over whether to push for a strongly universalistic versus a more targeted system (Christa Freiler, Brigitte Kitchen, personal interviews). Nevertheless, by the early 1990s a critical mass of social policy and anti-poverty groups had become aligned with the child poverty campaign, and Campaign 2000 claimed a membership in 1997 of forty-nine organizations (including core national social policy organizations; Popham, et al., 1997). A new more moderate coalition of groups focused on promoting a 'children agenda' would form and become relatively favoured by government as the decade wore on (Phillips, 2001).

The movement was relatively successful in building momentum within government to address children's issues, although international pressures contributed to this as well. Efforts by child poverty organizations culminated in the passing of an all party resolution in the House of Commons to eliminate child poverty by the year 2000 (also, ostensibly, a gesture to departing NDP leader Ed Broadbent). Internationally, both the participation of Canada in the 1990 World Summit for Children (in which Canada became committed to preparing an Action Plan for Children) and the December 1991 ratification of the United Nations Convention on the Rights of the Child pushed the Tory government into adopting a 'children's agenda.' Child poverty became the subject of both Senate and House of Commons committees who reported in

1991 and 1993 respectively.[24] In February 1992 the Mulroney government announced (in lieu of a national child care strategy, as some
commentators have observed) an initiative ('Brighter Futures') to fund
and develop programs for 'children at risk' (Canada, Health and Welfare Canada, 1992), and in May 1992 it introduced legislation (Bill C-80)
to reform 'child benefit' programs. By the early and mid-1990s the
federal Liberals and provincial governments had likewise been won
over to the idea of revising the child benefit system. 'Tackling child
poverty' was one of the two main goals put forward by the (Axworthy)
social security review discussion paper (in this case the connection
between child poverty and parental unemployment *was* acknowledged),
and improvements to child benefits and 'taking children off welfare'
became a central issue for discussion in the early and mid-1990s between federal and provincial governments. Children would, of course,
continue to be the focus of policy initiatives through the 1990s and into
the next debate, while both the 1999 and 2000 federal budget speeches
were billed as 'children's budgets.'

**Feminism Sidelined**

At its least progressive, as in the Tory approach, the child poverty issue
was placed within an individualizing discourse in which parents were
blamed, and the connection between the poverty of children and the
unemployment or underemployment of their parents was denied. In
this case, it served as a cover for a neo-liberal agenda of reduced social
spending and the dismantling of universal rights (including, ironically,
child benefits). At its most progressive, as in the platform of CPAG and
its allies who called for social responsibility for children, a national
child care system, affirmative action, pay equity, job creation, training,
full employment, and so on, the focus on child poverty seemed to be
compatible with the goals of socialist feminism. Most importantly, it
seemed to challenge the single male-breadwinner brand of familialism
promoted at this time by right-wing politicians and REAL Women
(Canada, Senate, Standing Committee on Social Affairs, Science and
Technology, 1989–90: (Group of Seven) 20: 25). Both versions, however,
share features that present a deeper problem from the standpoint of
women and the possibilities for a strong feminist voice. Indeed, both
versions express a vision and language that are profoundly family-
centred and gender-blind and give little visibility to women as an
identity. CPAG's vision and policy solutions, for example, rested on a

conceptualization of a 'life-cycle' consisting only of the gender-neutral stages of childhood, prospective parenthood, and parenthood (Canada, House of Commons Standing Committee on Human Resources Development, 1994: (CPAG) 7: 128). The main categories of concern were families, parents, and children. Even affirmative action and pay equity were framed as remedies for *families*, not women: 'We would ... like to recommend ... equity in affirmative action program ... If more and more women are entering the workforce, particularly in order to earn a second income for the family and thereby keep the family from poverty, it does not make sense that those women are not earning a sufficient wage to ensure that actually happens. Since this is obviously a family goal, it would be good if society could match that goal by ensuring that the wages that women earn have real value to the family' (Canada, Senate, Standing Committee on Social Affairs, Science and Technology, 1989–90: (Group of Seven) 20: 25). Within this discourse, gender was often ignored as a structural variable that contributes to poverty (e.g., CPAG, 1991). For example, to the extent that single mothers were still visible as a category of poor, their poverty tended to be presented in gender-blind terms, as yet another type of family poverty (e.g., Campaign 2000, 1992, 1994, 1995; CPAG, 1991).

With the adoption of child poverty as an official focus, women and gender concerns were effectively excised from the poverty story and the national debate on poverty and child benefits, and with this the opportunities for feminists to make claims on behalf of women in these debates were significantly reduced. These effects are visible in two conjunctural moments in the early 1990s. The first was the 1992 hearings on Bill C-80 – legislation that eliminated universality (the Family Allowance) from family benefits and instituted a more targeted system. The proposed legislation and ensuing discussion were framed entirely in terms of 'child poverty': women were no longer on the table. Thus, one of the selling points for this legislation used by the Department of Finance and other federal officials was that putting benefits on the basis of *family income* would be fairer to children and was a fairer way to determine family need:[25]

There is no question that family income is a more equitable basis for directing assistance to children. (Canada, Parliament, House of Commons, 1992: (John McDermid, for the Minister of Finance) 13217)

Family income has been widely regarded as being a better measure of a family's needs for child benefits. (Canada, Senate, Standing Committee on

Social Affairs, Science and Technology, 1992–3: (Ian Bennett, Senior Assistant Deputy Minister, Tax Policy Branch, Department of Finance) 21: 12

Under the new system, benefits will be based on family income, which is a better measure of a family's resources. This will ensure that benefits are directed on the basis of need. (1992–3: John Horton McDermid, Minister of State (Finance and Privatization)) 23: 9)

Likewise, some progressive social policy analysts supported this change: 'One of the advantages I see of the proposals ... is that they will put the child benefit system on a fairer and more consistent family income basis ... I think [it] is a good thing and a step forward' (Canada, House of Commons Legislative Committee on Bill C-80, 1991–92: (Ken Battle, Caledon Institute) 2: 7). These arguments were put forward without any reference to the long-time feminist claim that family-based eligibility criteria disproportionately deny benefits to women.

The opposition to this plan was dominated by social policy organizations focusing on the issue of child poverty and the problems of families and children (and would soon include a focus on the child development needs of young children[26]). While women's organizations disputed the simplistic focus on children (e.g., CACSW, 1990b), they made some movement to accept these terms in order, they judged, to participate at all in the defence of universality and the principle of social responsibility for children and to advocate for a strong federal presence in income security programs. It was a moment in which even feminists seemed temporarily to abandon women in favour of addressing the needs of gender-neutral families and children. Some of NAC's presentations on Bill C-80, for example, focused on the issue of child poverty (e.g., Canada, Senate, Standing Committee on Social Affairs, Science and Technology, 1992–3: (NAC) 22: 120; Canada, House of Commons Legislative Committee on Bill C-80, 1991–2: (NAC) 6: 35, 37), and their opposition to the elimination of universality and horizontal equity was expressed as a concern on behalf of families, rather than women, for example, 'families' costs of raising children' (Canada, House of Commons Legislative Committee on Bill C-80, 1991–2: (NAC) 6: 37; my emphasis). Key women's groups also seemed to relinquish their long-standing concern regarding individual entitlement for women: while some grassroots groups took the opportunity of these hearings to argue that the economic independence provided by the Family Allowance offered a life-saving buoy to women and children who were susceptible to violence in the home and that its loss would increase their risk (e.g., 1991–2: (RAIF), 16/7/92, 8: 46; York, 1992), national women's organizations such as NAC, the CACSW, and NAWL did not touch the issue. The latter groups presented the Family Allowance as money for children and families without reference to its special significance for women (Canada, House of Commons Legislative Committee on Bill C-80, 1991–2: (NAC) 6: 32).

The 1994 social security review hearings led to a further eclipsing of women and gender issues from the debates on poverty and social welfare policy. The child poverty issue fit comfortably with the Liberals' overall preference for an active rather than passive social policy strategy with its emphasis on encouraging people (especially single mothers) to move from welfare to a job. 'Reducing child poverty' was established by the HRDC discussion document as a central goal of reform, erasing all traces of the former discourse on 'women and poverty.' Although the latter discourse had, in typical liberal fashion, placed the blame for women's poverty at the foot of gender socialization (i.e., poverty was because women were raised with the expectation that they would be financially supported for life by men), it had at least made visible the disadvantages women experienced in the labour market and their added burden of unpaid domestic and care work. The discussion paper conveyed the image of gender-neutral parents who were expected to be self-supporting for the sake of the children.[27] There was no acknowledgment that single mothers faced more barriers than any other able-bodied adults in their quest for self-reliance. Their low wages or lack of decent jobs were being diagnosed as the result of a lack of education, training, and work experience. The focus on child poverty thus helped to rationalize a shift towards gender-neutral thinking, or as Janine Brodie terms it, 'phallocentricity,' in which the existence of 'difference' was denied altogether and equality was simply assumed (Brodie, 1996a: 134–5).

This is not to say that women's groups were primarily silenced or depoliticized by these events. With the theme of poverty no longer affording a focus on women in these debates, women's groups and their leftist allies turned to another discursive strategy, that of defining their claims in the language of 'equality,' underscoring the threat that the withdrawal of public social programs and social services and the lack of decent jobs posed to women's independence. 'Equality,' not 'poverty,' became the keyword in feminist presentations during both the 1992 and 1994 hearings:[28]

I will not limit my comments to the substance of Bill C-80, but shall talk about social programs in a broader context and particularly the impact of the erosion of social programs for women. It is our view that the changes to the system of children's benefits must be seen in the broader context of women's *equality*. (Canada, Senate, Standing Committee on Social Affairs, Science and Technology, 1992–3: (NAC) 22: 120; my emphasis)

There has to be a commitment to creating equality in this country. Social programs play a critical role in creating equality, particularly for women. Women's equality needs to be central in considering any review of social policy in this country. (Canada, House of Commons Standing Committee on Human Resources Development, 1994: (NAC) 4: 15)

This shift in focus reflected the broader recognition that neo-liberal discourse was denying legitimacy to the values of equality and social justice. This current inspired the 1996 'Women's March Against Poverty' that was jointly organized by NAC and the CLC. The march was not a return to the 'feminization of poverty' interpretation with its connotation of women as victims, but rather was an attempt to broaden the discussion on social policy to take account of the structural conditions (e.g., high unemployment) and policy shifts (neo-liberal offloading of federal responsibility for social programs, the attacks on the UI program, the failure to introduce a national child care program, and so on) that were contributing to women's inequality and poverty. As the analysis here suggests, however, the focus on equality was not merely a creative response to the new political conditions or a necessary counterpoint to neo-liberalism's disavowal of the values of equality and justice. It was also a fall-back position for feminism – a desperate attempt to reinsert 'women' into the equation and, at the same time, a retreat to a more generic claim, given the ideological closures that were built into the discourse on child poverty.

But apart from the broad backlash against feminism created by neo-liberalism, the focus on equality did not mesh well with the claims that continued to be made in the late 1990s by mainstream social policy groups on the reform of child and family benefits. By then the women's movement was no longer even considered a serious player in these policy discussions and was perceived by *both* government and left-liberal actors as radical, adversarial – and irrelevant.[29] This situation was certainly apparent at the time of the 1996 Women's March, an event that was largely ignored by the federal government and the media, while certain progressive groups viewed it as 'coming out of left field' and having no connection with the 'real' issues (Christa Freiler, personal interview). Moreover, groups that adopted a child poverty focus gained considerable credibility as experts on poverty – and even on the *gender impact* of poverty (illustrated, for example, in the allocation of funding by Status of Women Canada to CPAG for a gender analysis of social support programs) (see, e.g., Freiler and Cerny, 1998; and Freiler et al., 2001). The absence of the feminist voice in the debates on poverty, income support, and child benefits, in turn, allowed many (but not all)[30] social policy analysts even within the progressive-liberal community to maintain a silence on women and to ignore gender as a variable. As feminist commentators pointed out, a feminist perspective was missing from the responses of this sector to the Axworthy discussion paper (e.g., Banting and Battle, 1994; Caledon Institute of Social Policy, 1994; 1995).[31] Feminist analysts have continued to note the absence of a focus on women in social policy and poverty discourse (e.g., Monica Townson, 2000; Wiegers, 2002; Rebick, 2000).[32] Nor does the more recent interest in 'social exclusion' by social policy actors hold much promise for renewing interest in women and gender (e.g., Luxton, 2002). This invisibility is only perpetuating a familialist and phallocentric approach to social policy and public policy.

Whereas in the early to mid-1980s key women's organizations were an integral part of the community of national social policy organizations seeking a progressive (mainly liberal, but where they could, universalistic and individualized) social policy framework, by the early 1990s this was no longer the case. The absence of feminist actors in this policy milieu has, in turn, only reinforced the invisibility of women in social policy and allowed a narrow, familialist (and liberal-individualist), and male-centred approach to policy to go unchallenged. This continues to be the case, despite the recent discourse on 'investing in the child' and current rhetoric on 'social exclusion / social cohesion,' the latter of which is seemingly still largely centred on the figure of the child and the issue of child poverty.[33] The point is that such changes need to be understood as the result of a complex interplay of processes taking place at both macro and policy community levels. Clearly, neoliberal plans for a narrower welfare state, deep cuts to the funding of women's organizations, and a broadening of the constituency of the movement all contributed to a radicalization of the women's movement and to its subsequent marginalization from the mainstream political community.

But the discursive conditions generated by, and shaping, mainstream social policy debate were another major conditioning factor. The strategic choice of the left-liberal sector to focus on the theme of child poverty had particularly far-reaching consequences for feminist agency in this policy terrain. While eliminating child poverty was and continues to be a commendable goal, this thrust has served strategically to reframe the discussion in gender-neutral (gender-blind) terms. Women were effectively 'written out' of the poverty problem, and women's organizations lost credibility as valuable or legitimate actors in social policy politics, although as 'outsiders' they continue, along with their allies on the left, to struggle to broaden the focus to a wider set of issues with regard to social justice and equality.

# CHAPTER SEVEN

# Conclusions: Implications for Current Struggles for Women-Friendly Social Policy

Despite the ambiguity of and debate surrounding the concept, dependency continues to be a central issue for women. Both the ideology and actuality of dependency continue to dictate a lesser citizenship status for women both within the family and wider society, consigning many women to a life of compulsory caring and economic vulnerability. The availability of and conditions of entitlement for income security benefits are key factors that have reinforced this status. Feminists have long been torn between pursuing the course of securing benefits for poor mothers and that of seeking entitlement for individuals qua individuals, ideally in the context of universalized programs. While both are important strategies for women, this book has specifically urged a rereading of the latter strategy of individualization. A central claim of this book is that the feminist campaign for individualized entitlement provided an important avenue for advancing a women-friendly, and indeed, more human-friendly, framework for social policy. The aim was not a liberal or neo-liberal construction of citizenship that ignores social context and social interdependence, but rather a model of citizenship based on the *social individual*. The model of society as advanced in this book recognizes the value of care work to society, together with the importance of individuality for political voice. This model values and encourages a sense of community and social citizenship.

This book has focused on the progress, or lack of progress, that feminists have made in this struggle. While Canadian feminists were primed to advance a politics of autonomy and individualization, which rested on a social-democratic and/or collectivized understanding of social policy, their efforts largely failed to blossom into an effective challenge to the familialist, targeting-the-poor, status quo. Although there were many barriers to success, I have focused on the fact that the core organizations of the women's movement ultimately lost faith in this strategy. They ceased to believe that it was an important or viable option for this policy field, even though they did continue to strive for individual entitlement in relation to a range of policy areas, including family law, rape, abortion, wife battering, rights for native women, and in other established insurance-based and universalistic programs such as Unemployment Insurance and pensions. These changes occurred as national women's organizations made choices on the issue of child benefits, and these choices were made within a decisional context clearly 'not of their making.'

The story began when the institutionalized women's movement emerged in the early 1970s with two primary orientations to social policy. On the one hand, feminist organizations favoured measures that collectivized social risks and aimed to achieve a more level playing field, modified by a concern to treat women as independent, autonomous individuals deserving of benefits on the basis of their own labour and contributions to society. Within the terms of the fairly well-developed national social policy system and commitment to social provision that existed at this time, feminists believed that programs that gave benefits to women as individuals were most valuable to women. On the other hand, they believed, along with other mainstream social policy actors, that it was important to address *vertical equity* (a concept that takes the family as the unit of analysis) or the problem of poverty. The balance within the women's movement tipped, however, in favour of the left-liberal so-called anti-poverty approach and was diverted from the social individual model. This was clearly the result, in part, of the particular ideological cast of liberal feminism and of the class character of the institutionalized women's movement itself. Throughout the 1970s and early 1980s the institutionalized women's movement was consistently drawn to the argument for individual entitlement to income support benefits, and it recognized this principle as an important one generally for women. Nevertheless, liberal feminists within the movement were reticent about applying this idea to income transfer programs for families with children. This position reflected their belief in the institution of heterosexual marriage, family, and children, a view that was evident in the RCSW report. These women's groups were not willing to prioritize independence *from* marriage over equity *within* marriage and the family. In the case of family benefits, the goal of individualized entitlement competed with another practical goal of liberal feminism and that was to establish the family as a *partnership* and to thereby ensure that *both* parents are held responsible for the care and upbringing of their children. Views of class also had an effect, with the (primarily liberal) feminists involved in the debate believing that autonomy and/or independent rights had more relevance for middle-class than for lower-class women. At a particular juncture, liberal feminists prioritized vertical equity over gender equity for family benefits, illustrating Maxine Molyneux's point, and the insights of post-structuralist feminism, that there is no such thing as universal women's interests; women's unity is always contingent on overcoming divisions of class, race, ethnicity, and so on.

Broad macro-level social, economic, and political conditions, including the prevailing universe of political discourse, also conditioned the policy environment within which feminists identified and framed their interests and made their policy choices. Beginning in the 1960s, the Canadian welfare state and dominant political regime turned towards a social liberal model that entailed a new openness towards the voices of civil society and a willingness to address issues of inequality. It was, nevertheless, a shift that privileged the idea of poverty, with its embedded message of targeting the disadvantaged, and it was to lay some of the foundations for the transformation to liberalism and later neo-liberalism. Material conditions also influenced feminist positions. Growing unemployment and poverty, and the increasing incidence of single mothers in poverty, underwrote a concern about poverty and a belief in targeting the poor. Government agendas were important in setting the overall tone for social policy debate. A political goal of retrenchment introduced in the mid-1970s, and the explicitly right-wing, neo-conservative orientation of the first-term Mulroney government, created a social policy climate that was generally hostile to the ideals of progressive social reform and universality, and it encouraged further acceptance of targeted and poverty-oriented measures. Belief in the provision of a safety net was further eroded in the early and mid-1990s under the second-term Conservatives, and then the Liberals. Progressive constituencies were forced in this era to defend the very principle of social provision and federal responsibility. A climate of antipathy to so-called special interest groups, which included drastic cuts to their funding, challenged the credibility and viability of institutionalized women's organizations as the voice of women. A context of economic recession, neo-liberal policy shifts, and especially threats to women's employment, encouraged institutional feminism to adopt a more oppositional brand of politics and to tend to veer away from a narrow focus on social security measures.

Changes to income support programs themselves also altered the political landscape in this field. This happened in a way that closed political space for mobilizing around the issue of women's individual entitlement. Such changes included the introduction of the targeted Child Tax Credit in 1978, which created a functional alternative to the Family Allowance. The CTC helped to obscure the horizontal equity role of the allowance and in general made defending the allowance more difficult. The partial de-indexing of the Family Allowance in the mid-1980s ensured that the value of the benefit would erode over time. Indeed, in 1989 the allowance was clawed back, which eliminated the principle of universality and introduced inconsistency in the treatment of one- versus two-earner families. Finally, the cancellation of the Family Allowance Programme in 1992 closed a political space that feminists had traditionally occupied in advancing an alternative vision for equality. In addition, the possibility for a feminist politics of autonomy in this policy terrain was diminished by the increasing dismantling of social programs in the late 1980s and early 1990s via a 'politics of stealth' and by the limited, targeted, and gender-blind nature of proposals for family support advanced in the mid-1990s.

Macro-level trends and broad institutional and policy shifts were not alone, however, in shaping feminist views and conditioning their choices in the field of child and family benefits policy and on the issue of poverty. Rather, there was an interplay between these features and the discursive universe within the social policy community itself. This is a universe to which a range of actors, from hegemonic state players to marginalized oppositional players, contribute and whose demands interact to shape the parameters of debate and the process of reform. While marginal to the policy-making inner circle, left-liberal social policy and anti-poverty organizations in particular left a distinctive mark on this realm of debate. Their interpretations of social problems, which were themselves creative responses to the broad social, economic, and political changes taking place, created a conceptual framework for making sense of the policy issues that severely circumscribed the claims-making space for the more marginalized feminist movement. Their constructions effectively drew the women's movement further into an anti-poverty framework in relation to child benefits policy.

An important turning point occurred in the mid-1970s as women were 'written in' to the poverty story. The category of women was included largely as a sub-type of *family* poverty. Women's poverty was seen largely as the poverty of single-parent families. This construction drew on and reinforced a liberal feminist focus on the plight of single mothers. It marked the beginning of a new hegemonic ideology concerning 'women and poverty' – an accomplishment indeed from the standpoint of taking gender into account – and a move that solidified an alliance, albeit an unequal one, between the mainstream antipoverty movement and the mainstream women's movement. But if this discourse signified success for the women's movement, it also narrowed its space for political manoeuvre. With this construction the institutionalized women's movement was captured by the view that women could make significant gains through income support measures that addressed family poverty, and it was within these terms that feminists chose to support the introduction in 1978 of the targeted Child Tax Credit Programme. The women's movement equated the needs of single mothers who would benefit from the program with the needs of women in general. This belief that 'what is good for the *poor* is good for *women*' was reaffirmed once more by mainstream feminism in its mid-1980s stand on child benefits.

These were also, of course, moments of relinquishment and closure for the goal of individualization and politics of autonomy. In 1978 the institutionalized women's movement made a policy choice that derailed, although not completely, the strategy of individualization for this policy area. Family-based entitlement was deemed as the normal rule for child- and family-oriented income support policy, while the women's movement continued to hold individual entitlement as a desirable and feasible option for insurance-based and universalistic programs (e.g., Unemployment Insurance, taxation, and Old Age Security).

The early 1980s presented new windows for advancing the issue of women's right to benefits based on their own work, including the debate on pensions for homemakers, but more particularly, the debate over the future of the Family Allowance Programme (although, even here, the money was for mothers, not women). 'Money in women's own name' became the mobilizing call of the early 1980s' feminist campaign to preserve the Family Allowance. This focus could not be sustained, however, given the developments of the mid-1980s. Institutionalized feminism was at this point an integral, yet marginal, constituency within the mainstream progressive camp of social policy organizations. It was drawn into a politics defined primarily by the prominent left-liberal social policy organizations, one that narrowly prioritized the goal of vertical equity and redistribution of income to the exclusion, largely, of the principles of universality and horizontal equity. It had implications as well for marginalizing the Family Allowance as a viable policy instrument. Thus, while feminists did indeed 'lose the battle' over the Family Allowance in the mid-1980s, they were clearly subject to subtle pressures to abandon this cause – pressures that existed by virtue of the particular preoccupations of their allies within the social policy community.

One response of the left-liberal policy community to the harsh neo-liberal sensibilities that emerged in the late 1980s was to create a new master story on poverty, this time centred on the child. While this was a creative attempt to contest neo-liberalism's strategy of targeting and downsizing, and to give poverty a human face, it had important negative repercussions for feminist agency. The problem was in the ideological closures that were built into the discourse on child poverty. Gender neutrality replaced gender specificity in the language of social policy. Children replaced single mothers as the deserving poor and a focus on child poverty replaced the one on women and poverty as a central public issue. The purging of gender and women (and indeed, of adults generally) from the definition of the problem of poverty was, like their earlier inclusion, a critical discursive event shaping women's interests and feminist politics on federal poverty policy. It effectively dissolved the political ground that feminism occupied in the field of federal income support policy, and it further shut down the feminist politics of autonomy in this policy field. Feminists were all but silent when the Family Allowance Programme was finally abolished in 1992. Clearly, then, the women's movement not only *withdrew* from the mainstream debate on child benefits on its own volition; its credibility as an actor in this policy terrain came under attack. The women's movement was further disempowered as the focus on child poverty allowed the debate to shift towards positions and a vocabulary that were family-centred and phallocentric, epitomized in the 1994 federal discussion paper on social security reform.

### The Broader Implications for Understanding Welfare State Politics

The findings of this book provide new insight into the political processes of welfare state restructuring in Canada. The Canadian welfare state has been fundamentally transformed in the past three decades, with the direction of change imprinted by the neo-liberal goals of reduced government responsibility for social programs, increased employment flexibility, increased individual responsibility for well-being, and increased targeting of benefits (McKeen and Porter, 2003). According to John Myles and Paul Pierson, the Canadian welfare state has undergone a 'paradigm shift,' one marked by the transition from a universal and insurance-based social security system to one based on income-tested and targeted benefits (1997). They argue that in the context of fiscal austerity, the new model of choice among policy-makers is the negative income tax / guaranteed income (NIT/GI) program in which income-tested and targeted income transfers are delivered through the tax system. There has also been a significant shift in the *subject* of social policy (Jenson, 2000; Jenson, Mahon, and Phillips, 2003). As Jane Jenson has argued, ideal-typical citizens are no longer the adult workers who gain access to income transfers and services on the basis of their status as workers and/or heads of households with dependent children, but rather, the children. In Canada, this reorientation is reflected in such new intitiatives as the National Child Benefit, the intergovernmental National Children's Agenda, and a range of new initiatives designed to address child development concerns. As Jane Jenson and Denis Saint-Martin argue, the new welfare state model in Canada, and across a range of industrialized nations, is increasingly geared to what is being called investing in human capital – an approach that emphasizes lifelong learning, equality of 'opportunity' as opposed to 'outcome,' and investing now in order to ensure the future – all articulated as investing in 'children,' especially young children (2002; also see Dobrowolsky and Saint-Martin, 2002). Access to social benefits for adults in Canada is increasingly conditional upon their having an attachment to a child (Jenson, 2000).

To understand the political dimensions of these shifts, however, we need to expand our research horizons beyond the standard approaches in political studies, including the predeterministic tendencies inherent in 'path dependency' theory, the simplistic notion that neo-liberalism resulted from political elites imposing change from above or through strategies characterized by stealth, and the focus on the 'usual political suspects' – that is, class actors and mainstream political organizations. For example, in examining the conditions that led to the shift towards a new targeting model for social security, Myles and Pierson (1997) note the importance of the support by a novel political coalition composed of two constituencies: (1) conservatives and business interests, who were pleased with the potential for retrenchment and the strengthening of work incentives, and (2) moderates and liberals, who were willing to 'acquiesce' to targeting because of its potential for increasing benefits for the poor. By focusing on struggles within the context of the social policy community, and struggle over the meaning or interpretations of problems, the present study supports Myles's and Pierson's acquiescence thesis and adds texture and nuance to this claim. It has shown that the political choices of left-liberal social policy and anti-poverty organizations, and women's organizations, though well-intentioned, effectively reinforced and legitimated the shift to targeting, particularly for the core area of child benefits. The nature of their influence has been both indirect and direct. Indirectly, the role of social policy organizations in shaping the discourse on poverty was significant. Rodney Haddow does indeed capture a key feature of the politics of Canadian social policy restructuring in describing it as a politics of poverty, although his work fails to interrogate poverty as a discourse that was socially constructed. The discursive turn in social policy discourse towards a renewed focus on poverty was critical in laying ideological foundations for a shift to an anti-poverty model. While poverty is not a false concept, and theoretically can lead either to social-democratic (universalistic and solidaristic) or liberal (targeting-the-poor) solutions, the reading advanced by mainstream anti-poverty activists in Canada has logically supported the liberal solution of giving benefits only to those deemed truly needy. The left-liberal social policy sector (in collaboration at different moments with women's and child poverty organizations) chose to build a focus on particular vulnerable groups (e.g., the elderly, women, single mothers, and children). This approach almost presupposes a targeting orientation that feeds into undermining a sense of social solidarity and collectivity that has been a key element in the neo-liberal agenda (McKeen and Porter, 2003).

Left-liberal organizations also directly supported the neo-liberal targeting thrust, as Myles and Pierson suggest. First, dominant left-liberal social policy organizations, and at various times key organizations of the women's movement, increasingly embraced the goal of enhancing the targeting of the system, something that was evident in their initial receptivity to the Child Tax Credit in the late 1970s, and especially in the mid-1980s' policy stands of the Social Policy Reform Group (SPRG). Proclaiming 'half a loaf was better than no loaf at all,' social policy groups moderated their support at this time for universality and horizontal equity and positioned themselves in favour of enhancing the targeted Child Tax Credit over the universal Family Allowance. It was an approach that, in retrospect, further legitimized a neo-liberal politics of austerity.

The left-liberal sector also had, and continues to have, both a direct and indirect influence in supporting targeting by promoting the issue of child poverty and collaborating on revamping social policy discourse and key programs around the figure of the child versus the adult citizen. Key social policy organizations seized upon the theme of child poverty as the weak link in the chain of neo-liberalism, and along with international influences, were at the forefront of the movement pressuring governments to take up the issue. While solving child poverty is a worthy goal, this focus served generally to provide a convenient political cover for governments bent on reducing social spending and increasing targeting. Under the Mulroney government, for instance, the rhetoric on child poverty was accompanied by deep cuts in child benefits and the elimination of universality. Moreover, while the Liberal focus on child-centred policy may have created new openings for progressive programming (in the area of child care for example; Jenson, Mahon, and Phillips, 2003), it has also potentially allowed governments to continue a neo-liberal targeting orientation towards 'fixing' children who are 'at risk' (McGrath, 1997), which is the antithesis of a preventative, solidaristic, and universalistic approach. The focus on child poverty helped to usher in a child-centred view of social policy and social citizenship in Canada in which 'investing in the child' – especially the young child, as child-development experts have encouraged – is becoming the primary objective (Jenson, 2000; Jenson, Mahon, and Phillips, 2003; Dobrowolsky and Saint-Martin, 2002; Jenson and Saint-Martin, 2002). While the hope of 'child poverty,' and recently, many 'social exclusion,' activists was, and still is, to eliminate child poverty, there has been little real progress to date. As analysts have shown, even with new spending on federal child benefits, these benefits remain relatively small and fall far short of addressing real needs (Wiegers, 2002; Stroick and Jenson, 1999; Durst, 1999; Pulkingham and Ternowetsky, 1999; McKeen, 2001), and poverty in Canada continues to grow (McKeen and Porter, 2003).

The analysis presented in this book has also provided a deeper understanding of the ways a range of more radical oppositional groups, notably the women's movement (in its socialist-feminist incarnation), labour organizations, and popular sector groups, were marginalized in debates on social policy in the mid-1980s to mid-1990s. The political voice and mobilizing capacities of labour and disadvantaged groups were undermined generally by the broad policy shifts and new state practices, to be sure. These shifts and practices included repressive work and labour legislation (Porter, 2003), steps that have closed off the access that these groups previously had to state actors (for instance, by removing advocates from within the state and reducing funding; Jenson and Phillips, 1996), and policies and practices that created or exacerbated societal divisions and explicitly targeted certain groups (Porter, 2003). The strategy of targeting, for example, as Janine Brodie has argued, played a key role in making structural differences and inequalities invisible, thereby pathologizing and individualizing differences: 'It disassembles and diffuses the collective claims of the women's movement, recasting it as a "ghetto of disadvantaged groups"' (1994: 74). As the present study shows, however, labour and social justice organizations were also marginalized as participants within *particular* social policy debates – a situation that was reinforced by the particular strategic and discursive choices of the more moderate progressive sector. Indeed, as I have shown, left-liberal social policy and anti-poverty organizations and, at times, liberal-minded women's organizations, often intervened in social policy debates in ways that effectively narrowed, rather than broadened, the scope of debate, and that contributed to a context that made it increasingly difficult for more radical voices to be heard. Just such a role was played by SPRG in the mid-1980s debate on child benefits. Constituencies such as labour, feminist movements, and popular sector groups organized under the Action (Pro-) Canada Network, and child poverty advocacy groups (in their earlier incarnation) actively rejected the Mulroney government's austerity agenda and offered alternative reform ideas that were grounded in the principles of universality, horizontal equity, full employment, and equality. Their presentations at public hearings, however, were readily dismissed in the face of SPRG's moderate and more supportive position on the Conservative's proposals. Similarly, in the case of the past decade of debate on child benefits, the language of child poverty with its predominantly gender-neutral and family-centred constructions played an insidious role in eliminating gender considerations from the debate and expelling the women's movement from this terrain. Their 'outsider' status was only further established as women's and labour groups attempted to broaden the social policy agenda to include economic and social justice issues – efforts that were seen by more mainstream actors as being at odds with, and irrelevant to, their own focus on child and family poverty. The role of 'moderates and liberals' in some sense, then, was something more than what Myles and Pierson have termed *acquiescence*.

Incorporating an analysis of policy community discourses broadens our understanding of political processes. It shows us that the activities of a wider range of political actors, both powerful and not so powerful, are significant as well in shaping political struggle and in influencing regime change. Progressives were clearly not to blame for neo-liberal restructuring, but neither were their political and strategic choices incidental to the processes whereby the neo-liberal paradigm came to dominate and more radical options were closed off. In sum, the particular political choices and strategies of maginalized actors have mattered, and do matter, in the shaping of new welfare state politics and paradigms.

### Policy Implications: Where We Go from Here?

Janine Brodie has contended that relations between the state and society are 'less directive than coterminous and discursive, embedded in our shared understandings of what is natural, neutral and universal' (1998: 27). If this be so, we must read the relinquishment of feminism's alternative vision for a key area of federal social policy as one aspect – one that is perhaps both cause and consequence – of the broader continuing failure of social policy-makers to take seriously issues of gender, social reproduction, and equality, as well as their failure to give credence to the feminist voice in the field. Guided by an agenda of withdrawing from and reprivatizing the provisions of social welfare, and shifting responsibility for meeting social need onto individuals and families, neo-liberal policy-makers have pushed forward an agenda of family-based entitlement for social policy, even with respect to programs that have always respected individual rights. Family-income testing was introduced into the unemployment insurance system (now Employment Insurance) in 1996 (for the first time its history), despite the fact that the women's movement had long lobbied against it.[1] While family-income testing only pertains to the 'top-up' portion of the family supplement component, analysts viewed it as the 'thin edge of the wedge' in terms of shifting to family-based eligibility, a step that would disproportionately eliminate women's eligibility for benefits (Pulkingham, 1998).[2] Family-based criteria were also to be used under the Seniors Benefit proposed in 1996 which, had it been implemented, would have replaced the individually based Old Age Security Programme and family-based Guaranteed Income Supplement. Similar shifts were also taken at the provincial level in the flurry of restructuring in the mid-1990s. The Conservative government of Ontario, for example, reinstated the 'spouse in the house' rule so that there is, again, an automatic assumption of mutual dependency when two adults who are not of the same sex live together. While left-leaning governments have had a more complex response to the issue of individualization, they have nevertheless tended to support the practice of family-based eligibility. For example, in the early 1990s the Ontario NDP government addressed this question in relation to social assistance benefits, recommending that social assistance continue to be based on family criteria (following the definitions in the Ontario Family Law Act), except where there was 'real need' caused by the spouse not providing support. It reasoned that dependencies should not be ignored where they exist and that an individual-based system would unfairly favour stay-at-home 'homemakers': 'Using a purely individual benefit unit would potentially have the effect of turning social assistance into a guaranteed annual income for every person in Ontario who stays at home and who has no personal income. It would become a homemaker's allowance, which would go mainly to women who stay home' (Ontario, Advisory Group on New Social Assistance Legislation, 1992: 51). Likewise, in addressing the question of whether tax-delivered benefits (e.g., Child Tax Credit) should be based on the individual or the family, the Ontario Fair Tax Commission appointed by the NDP government concluded that using the individual as the basis of policy would undermine the integrity of programs aimed at *vertical equity* (Ontario, Fair Tax Commission, 1992: 8, 16).

This backlash against the concept and cause of independence for women in the context of social policy has also played out within the women's movement itself. Women's groups were outraged at the introduction of a two-tier benefit structure (based on familial dependencies) in the Unemployment Insurance Programme and at the 1994 suggestion that UI be based on family income ('We find it deplorable that the government has attempted to portray this reactionary measure as a benefit for single mothers'; Canada, House of Commons Standing Committee on Human Resources Development, 1994: (NAC), 25/2/94).[3] Nevertheless, women's groups articulated the problem as mainly pertaining to the issue of domestic violence against women and as an intrusion into, and the regulation of, women's private lives (reminiscent of how the argument changed in relation to the Family Allow-ance), and not as an issue affecting all women, or as a core principle of equality (e.g., ibid., 1994: (NAWL) 35: 113, 114; 9: 191; (CACSW) 28: 8; (NAC) 25/2/94). Nor did feminists demonstrate strong opposition to the family-income–testing aspect of the proposed Seniors Benefit. The absence of debate over these initiatives contrasts sharply with situa-tions taking place in many European countries where the question of individualized versus family-based (or 'derived') benefits has been a relatively controversial topic since the European Economic Community's directive in the mid-1980s to encourage governments to move towards individualized entitlement to social security (McKeen, 1994b; Luckhaus, 1994).

The failure to effectively oppose familialization and to establish an alternative non-sexist vision for social policy was one element that allowed conditions to emerge that have made it relatively easy for neo-liberal reformers to refuse to take issues of women and gender equality seriously, and to move the system as a whole away from a women-friendly model. Canada's system of social support became narrowed, and it is now primarily structured to encourage the growth of low wages and insecure employment (i.e., part-time, temporary, lacking in benefits; McKeen and Porter, 2003). Women, especially, have been af-fected by these changes. Their access to UI/EI has been reduced while the amount of the benefit has also dropped (Porter, 2003; MacDonald, 1998; Phipps, et al., 2001). Many social assistance regimes have been reformed in ways that have reduced access to benefits for single moth-ers, often forcing them off welfare and into workfare and poor jobs (MacDonald, 1998; Evans, 1996; Scott, 1996; Baker and Tippen, 1999; Vosko, 2000).[4] Child benefits reform has reinforced women's depen-dency through the shift from universal to family-based entitlement, and it has failed to alleviate the poverty of the poorest women and their children (MacDonald, 1998; McKeen, 2001).

The pressure and poverty women are experiencing on a daily basis has been escalating. They have been increasingly forced to juggle the load of unpaid care work with low-paid, contingent employment, or to choose between finding (or returning) to a 'husband' male-breadwin-ner or taking workfare or low wage, short-term employment (Vosko, 2000). Single mothers, who have the most difficulty in living up to these impossible demands, have often been easy targets for blame (Swift and Birmingham, 1999; Wiegers, 2002). All of this has implications for the ability of women to exercise political voice or to engage publicly. Caught in a cycle of low-wage, contingent work and unpaid care work, many women, especially time- and money-pressed single mothers and racialized and minority women, do not have the resources and support that would allow them to be politically active. At the same time, confronted with the overwhelming focus on child poverty, child development, and social exclusion (for many, also to be read as child poverty and child development), the Canadian women's movement and its allies on the left are struggling to find even a *language* to advance notions of gender equality and social justice.

Feminist politics of autonomy and struggle for individualized entitlement was once at the cutting edge of a broader vision for social policy, resting on the values of the collectivity, community, and individual autonomy. It failed to flourish within the sphere of the federal debate on poverty. Nevertheless, this vision needs to be pursued if we are to solve the issues of inequality (gender and other forms of inequality) and work towards a model of society that is more humane and solidaristic. Social programs should offer women a genuine alternative to marriage and the family through an ability to form autonomous households. They should go beyond this, however, to create conditions that allow women, and everyone, to have a sense of belonging and community, for these are also essential ingredients of full citizenship. Ultimately, such conditions are only achievable within a system that puts the *social individual* at the centre of policy, that is, within a system that recognizes the inextricable interconnection between the ability of adults to work for pay, to care for loved ones and dependents, and to participate politically in order to influence the policies and conditions that affect them.

# Appendix: List of Interviews

The following is a list individuals interviewed for this research project, including the organizations they were associated with during the periods under study, and the location and date of the interview. All interviews were tape-recorded.

Bob Baldwin – Canadian Labour Congress. Ottawa, 7 July 1997.

Ken Battle – National Welfare Council, Caledon Institute of Social Policy, Social Policy Reform Group. Ottawa, 4 August 1997.

Louise Dulude – Canadian Advisory Council on the Status of Women, the National Action Committee on the Status of Women, Social Policy Reform Group. Ottawa, 30 June and 7 July 1997. (Questions and answers were exchanged via fax.)

Margrit Eichler – Ontario Institute for Studies in Education. Toronto, 18 June 1997.

Christa Freiler – Child Poverty Action Group. Toronto. 18 June 1997.

Robert Glossop – Vanier Institute of the Family. Ottawa, 27 June 1997.

Terrence Hunsley – Canadian Council on Social Development, Social Policy Reform Group. Ottawa, 2 June 1997.

Martha Jackman – National Association of Women and the Law. Ottawa, 30 May 1997.

Patrick Johnston – National Anti-Poverty Organization, Canadian Council on Social Development, Social Policy Reform Group. Toronto, 18 June 1997.

Brigitte Kitchen – Child Poverty Action Group. Toronto, 19 June 1997.

Ruth Rose Lizée – National Action Committee on the Status of Women; Fédération des Femmes du Québec. Montreal, 28 August 1997.

Janet Maher – National Action Committee on the Status of Women. Toronto, 19 June 1997.

Lorraine Michael – National Action Committee on the Status of Women. Toronto, 17 June 1997.

Rosemarie Popham – Campaign 2000. Toronto, 17 June 1997.

David Ross – Canadian Council on Social Development. Ottawa, 24 June 1997.

Lynn Toupin – National Anti-Poverty Organization. Ottawa, 25 June 1997.

Monica Townson – Canadian Advisory Council on the Status of Women. Toronto, 19 June 1997.

# Notes

## 1 Solutions for Women-Friendly Social Policy

1 Feminists also point out that the mainstream, gender-blind, social rights and decommodification concept within the power resources school of thought ignores differences in the situations of men and women with respect to paid and unpaid work, and therefore, presents a misleading account of men's situation. Men are not only decommodified by public benefits, they are also decommodified by the unpaid work of wives, mothers, and daughters, and men and women are affected differently by benefits that decommodify (e.g., parental leave may actually reduce a working women's earning capacity because of foregone increases in wages; Orloff, 1993).

2 Also see Lister (1995). O'Connor (1993) and others also note that personal autonomy, especially within families, requires a strong guarantee at both the formal and practical levels of sexual and bodily protection and rights.

3 Also see Lister (1995) and Lewis (1997). One advantage of this formulation is that it considers the structuring of civil and social rights to people as 'receivers' as well as 'givers' (of care) within the family.

4 Lewis has promoted the idea that women should have the choice *not* to engage in paid work (decommodification); the choice to do unpaid work; the choice to do paid work; and the choice not to engage in unpaid work (1997). Others have questioned the political feasibility of this vision (Orloff, 1997; Hobson, 1994).

5 According to Maxine Molyneux, 'practical gender interests' are interests that women (or men) share by virtue of their positioning within the existing gender division of labour. If realized, they would improve the material situation of some women but would not necessarily fundamentally chal-

lenge the gender order. 'Strategic gender interests' are deduced from feminist analyses of women's subordination and the belief that emancipation is possible (1985).

## 2  Understanding How the Interests of New Political Actors Are Shaped

1  See, e.g., Sue Findlay (1997); also see Gillian Walker (1990a; 1990b).

2  See, e.g., Bashevkin, 1998; Brodie, 1995; 1996a; 1998; and Gotell, 1998.

3  Yeatman also stresses that the state has at the same time developed various rationing strategies with regard to claims and claimants, including, e.g., the discourse of more effective 'targeting' of social welfare, or by devolving authority to units closer to the front line (meaning that claims and claimants are brokered much lower down the line, so that it is more difficult for them to elaborate their claims into generalized and generally visible discourses), or by producing elaborate discourses of change that are only window dressing and eat up the energies of advocates of change within these milieux (1990: 172).

4  This case also illustrates another of Yeatman's points – that the meanings of policies are determined by the logic of more dominant discourses (1990: 158). The primary response to the problem of child poverty by the Tories surely reflected the dominant Conservative discourse of individualization – i.e., that the cause of, and solutions to, social problems lie in the individual.

5  Yeatman stresses that part of challenging dominant discourse is being able to problematize the problem-setting frameworks embedded in official discourses, to mobilize around the contradictions and make them a site of struggle (1990: 166).

6  Jenson has criticized new social movement theory in general for its lack of attention to power (1994: 65).

7  With regard to state actors, structuralism-institutionalism perceives as important the autonomy they have from societal groups, and their capacity to draw on sufficient institutional resources to affect policy design and implementation. With regard to societal interests, the level of organizational development is important; the better developed an associational system is, i.e., the degree to which 'representative, well-resourced, autonomous, and policy-capable associational systems exist to articulate the interests of private actors within the sector' (Coleman and Skogstad, 1990: 313), the better equipped it is to act as a policy participant as opposed to policy advocate.

8  As it is defined within structuralism-institutionalism, the 'sub-

government' is the inner core of policy-makers – usually primar
government agencies but it can also include certain institutional
interest groups which have substantial resources and the capability of
interacting on a day-to-day level with government. The 'attentive public'
includes government agencies, private institutions, pressure groups, and
individuals who are interested in influencing certain policies but lack the
power of the inner core and do not participate in policy-making.

9 It should be noted that the exclusion of the feminist voice within
   Haddow's work also reflects the premise (shared with mainstream welfare
   state theory) that poverty politics is a class-based phenomenon, and only
   class-based actors are relevant (Haddow, 1993: 11–16).

10 I am indebted to Rianne Mahon for this key point.

## 3 The Mainstream Poverty Debate in the 1960s

1 The discovery of poverty was also made, for instance, in the United States,
   Britain, and Sweden.

2 Podoluck also served as the consultant on poverty for the RCSW.

3 'The combined financial resources of the family unit, rather than the
   income of individual family members, determine the level of living which
   can be achieved by the family' (Podoluk, 1968: 1).

4 For example, the Canadian Welfare Council produced several reports on
   family desertion (1925; 1941; 1956; 1961, and 1968). The discourse on the
   family was perpetuated through the 1970s and 1980s publications of
   CCSD and the Vanier Institute of the Family.

5 The high visibility of welfare mothers is evident, e.g., in Canada Parliament, Special Senate Committee on Poverty (1971), and Schlesinger (1972).

6 Rianne Mahon has similarly argued that the 'rediscovery of poverty' cast a
   shadow over the social policy reforms from the mid-1960s on, with programs targeted to the poor gaining a new popularity and derailing the
   drive for universality (1997: 23).

7 Many on the political left were critical of such organizations as CCSD,
   which they viewed as having been co-opted by the state and 'serv[ing] to
   sustain the illusion of meaningful debate and to reinforce the very narrow
   ideological space within which that debate occurs' (Loney, 1977: 458).

8 Five hundred delegates attended the Poor People's Conference, including
   350 welfare rights organizations (Walker, 1971).

9 Conferences included, e.g., the Nuffield Seminar organized by the CWC,
   and a 1974 conference sponsored by CCSD on income supplementation
   (at which the federal Minister of Health and Welfare Marc Lalonde partici-

pated; CCSD (1974). Studies of these organizations included, e.g., CWC (1969); CCSD, (1972, 1974); and NCW (1971, 1973, 1976).

10 As an example of overt discrimination, public housing at this time only allowed 2% of their clientele to be single mothers (Adams, 1970).

11 'Absence of husband' was used as an explanation of this type of poverty; see Report of the Federal–Provincial Study Group on Alienation (1971). The poverty of single mothers was considered to be natural and normal, given the absence of a male breadwinner. Podoluk's study, e.g., reflects no greater concern for or surprise about the poverty of female single parents than it does for families with aged heads (1968).

12 Welfare rights groups of the mid-1970s to early 1980s also believed in the naturalness and sanctity of the family, especially motherhood and the natural instincts of women to protect their own: 'All children need and have a right to remain with their natural mother, where they would experience a natural home environment, with brothers and sisters around them and a mother at the helm, loving them and doing it in a way that only a natural mother can' (Mother-Led Union, n.d.: 2). Their newsletters were especially concerned with the plight of the children of sole-support mothers on social assistance: 'When these mothers become frustrated with seeking and not finding employment, and not being able to raise their families the way they truly believe they should be raised, the government risks the very real possibility of an increase in emotional and physical child abuse' (Mother's Action Group, 1982: 15).

13 Similar views on poverty can be found in, e.g., *The Pedestal* (1971), James (1968), and Leueen (1971).

14 For similar views, see Goldfield, et al. (1972) and Morton (n.d.).

15 I have argued elsewhere, e.g., that Wages for Housework campaigners were instrumental in pushing liberal feminist organizations into becoming more attentive to social welfare policy issues such as the Family Allowance (McKeen, 1994a).

16 I will use 'NAC' rather than 'the NAC,' as this is the conventional way it is referred to.

17 The RCSW used presentations made by poor women to the Croll Committee, as very few of these groups presented briefs to the RCSW. Some sharing of information between the two committees seems evident: The Croll Committee and RCSW had one in camera session on 19 February 1970 (which was not recorded), and I found several briefs to the RCSW in the archival file of the Croll Committee.

18 Increasing divorce rates in the 1960s contributed to the rapid growth in the number of single-parent families. In 1961, one-parent families made up

8.4% of all families; in 1971 they represented 9.4% of families, and the overwhelming majority of the new single-parent families were headed by women (Boyd et al., 1976: 19).

19  The conventional approach to counting women's poverty was to count women who were husbandless. Poor families were generally encompassed under 'men's poverty' (Adams, 1970: 62). One exception (apart from the RCSW report) was Ian Adam's radical book, *The Poverty Wall* (1970), albeit it focused on single mothers only.

20  Also see Podoluk (1968: 130). The strong identification of women 'as mothers' is evidenced in a heading used in a table in the Croll Report: 'combined incomes of mother and husband' (Canada, Parliament, Special Senate Committee, 1971: 158).

21  My use of the term *social individualism* is borrowed from Celia Winkler's work (1998).

## 4  Feminism, Poverty Discourse, and the Child Benefits Debate

1  In the mid-1970s, Marc Lalonde announced at a CCSD conference that the federal government would be proceeding with plans for an income supplementation plan the details of which would be finalized by 1978 (CCSD, 1976a: 21–33).

2  International Women's Year and the funding provided by the Women's Programme of the Department of Secretary of State were important to the formation and operation of several new national groups, including the Canadian Research Institute for the Advancement of Women, MATCH (an agency to promote women and international development), the Canadian Congress for Learning Opportunities for Women, and the Canadian Association for the Advancement of Women and Sport. Also, native women founded the Native Women's Association of Canada in 1973 (Phillips, 1991: 763–4).

3  The Office of the Co-ordinator was given departmental status in 1976, with a mandate to report to the Minister Responsible for the Status of Women. By 1979 it was being called Status of Women Canada (Findlay, 1988).

4  NAC's new executive in April 1977 reflected both socialist-feminists (e.g., Marjorie Cohen, Laurel Ritchie, Lynn Kaye) and radical feminists (e.g., Lorenne Clark; Vickers et al., 1993: 85).

5  The relationship between the CACSW and the broader women's movement in this period was very different from that of the 1980s (Burt, 1998).

6  For example, key individuals included Louise Dulude (lawyer and tax

expert with the CACSW and NAC) and Monica Townson (an economist with CACSW).

7  By the same token, feminists criticized the assumption and practice of defining single-parent mothers on welfare as 'unemployable' and therefore not eligible for services such as child care and training that would assist them in finding paid work (Daly, 1975).

8  On the subject of joint taxation, see CACSW (1976b; 1977b), NAC (1978a), Dulude (1979), and Blain (1979).

9  This formulation originated with the Manitoba Volunteer Committee on the Status of Women in its 1968 brief to the RCSW. That marriage laws be changed to ensure women an equal share of the family income during marriage was indeed a major focus of organizations such as the CACSW and NAC (e.g., NCW, 1979a; 1983).

10  In 1979 the Liberal government tightened eligibility to UI benefits that especially affected part-time workers, re-entrants, new entrants, and repeaters, and therefore had an enormous impact on women.

11  The 'universality versus selectivity' debate would emerge in a more specific form in the mid-1980s with the coming to power of the Mulroney Tory government.

12  According to one informant, NAPO was initially opposed to the introduction of the credit because it was to be financed by reducing the Family Allowance by $5 a month, but it decided later to support it, 'once they understood that low income people and women would be further ahead' (Ken Battle, personal interview).

13  CCSD published three 'fact books' between 1975 and 1983, and it has continued to do so into the 1990s and 2000s (CCSD, 1975a, 1979b, 1983, 1989, 1994, 2000).

14  The reports were similar in approach: they presented data on the extent of poverty among the designated group, covered various aspects of the problem, expanded on the problems with existing services and the welfare system, and then criticized the social security review or the most recent government proposal, and ended with CCSD's own reform ideas on behalf of the vulnerable group being profiled.

15  *Women and Poverty* was revised by Louise Dulude in 1990. (See NCW, 1990b.)

16  Dulude's consciousness about poverty was raised during the time that she was employed for an organization working on behalf of poor people in Montreal (personal interview). According to Ken Battle, Dulude had to fight for the wording of the document, which was considered by Health and Welfare bureaucrats to be too 'anti-male' (personal interview).

17  As a proportion of all families, dual-earner families rose from 14% to 49% between 1961 and 1981 (Status of Women Canada, 1986: 7).

18  Female-headed families constituted 13.2% of total low-income families in 1961, but 28.7% in 1973, with the percentage almost doubling between 1967 and 1973 (CCSD, 1975a: 14). Single mothers also substantially increased their share in the population of poor women, from 7% to 18% of all poor women between 1971 and 1988 (Evans, 1991: 173).

19  The CACSW prepared a number of reports in the 1970s that focused on the one-parent family: in April 1974 it established a working group to examine the position of the one-parent family and pressed the federal government for a public policy paper on the one-parent family; in May 1976, it issued a position paper; and in January 1977, a document was issued outlining principles and recommendations on the one-parent family. Articles on the female single parent also appeared regularly in the grassroots feminist newsletters, such as *Kinesis* (published by the Vancouver Status of Women).

20  For example, see Lalonde's speech quoted in NCW (1976a: 14–15).

21  According to Dulude, the issue of women and poverty was picked up and promoted especially by provincial status of women councils (personal interview).

22  A similar focus on the poverty of elderly women is found, e.g., in NAC (1982, 1983); and CACSW (n.d., *Women and Aging*).

23  Bégin reported that, '87 per cent of all single parent families will receive some credit benefits' (Canada, House of Commons, 1978: 883) and that, in all, $30 million more would be going to single-parent families (1978: 1686).

24  It was generally reported that the CTC would go to women (e.g., NCW, 1979a). In actual fact, wives would only receive a credit if family income was below the threshold level and the credit was higher than taxes owed by the husband. The full amount of the credit at this time was $200 per child under age eighteen.

## 5 Feminism and the Tory Child Benefits Debate of the Early to Mid-1980s

1  Liberal proposals to improve public pensions were modest: increases to the selective Guaranteed Income Supplement, but no increases to CPP benefits and no introduction of homemakers pensions (Prince, 1984).

2  Political analysts have noted the initial openness and consensus-building orientation of the first term of the Tory government (e.g., Bashevkin, 1996: 216).

3  Venues for the debate on child benefits, included the following: the House

of Commons Standing Committee on Health, Welfare and Social Affairs (hearings held in March 1985, and reported in April 1985); the Senate Committee on Social Affairs, Science and Technology (hearings in May and June 1985; reported in December 1985 and June 1987); the House of Commons Legislative Committee on Bill C-70, an act that de-indexed family allowances (hearings held September 1985); the Senate Committee on Social Affairs, Science and Technology (hearings on Bill C-70 held November 1984 to March 1985). Debate on child benefits also spread into hearings on taxation, e.g., the House of Commons Standing Committee on Finance and Economic Affairs (hearings held December 1986 and fall 1987; reported November 1987); child poverty, e.g., the House of Commons Standing Committee on National Health and Welfare (hearings held December 1987); and the Goods and Services Tax, e.g., Finance Committee (hearings held late 1989).

4 Changes taking place in provincial policy also reflected the individual responsibility and dual-earner family model. For example, in the early 1980s the Ontario government began to declare sole-support mothers eligible for family benefits only if they sought employment, and in 1982 it established an employment support program for them (Haddad, 1985). This approach was also reflected in the federal government's 1987 proposal for CPP survivor benefits, which denied benefits to women with children over age seven with the view that these women should be self-supporting.

5 Changes in child benefits were announced in the 1985 and 1986 federal budgets, the June 1987 White Paper on Tax Reform, the December 1987 National Strategy on Child Care, and the 1988 and 1989 federal budgets.

6 The 1985 budget limited the indexing of personal exemptions and tax brackets as well as child benefit programs, and it partially de-indexed federal transfers to the provinces for health and education under the Established Programs Financing (EPF) mechanism. The 1986 budget imposed a general surtax of 3% on all personal incomes and corporations, reduced tax rates for businesses, and increased the federal sales tax. The 1988 budget introduced massive changes in the personal income tax structure that entailed reducing the number of tax brackets and reducing the tax rate for top income earners (Gray, 1990).

7 Among the organizations of minority women that emerged in the early and mid-1980s were the following: Congress of Black Women (established in 1980), Inuit Women's Association or Pauktuutit (established in 1984), and National Organization of Immigrant and Visible Minority Women (established in 1986; Phillips, 1991: 764).

8  The DisAbled Women's Network was formed in 1985 (Phillips, 1991: 764).

9  Sylvia Bashevkin emphasizes that NAC's tradition of compromise and consensus moderated the strains within it in the mid-1980s between protest-oriented feminists who took an oppositional approach to the Tories and more moderate, lobby-oriented feminists (1996: 222).

10  Louise Dulude also held the positions of vice-president (1984–5) and president (1986–8) of NAC.

11  Two key figures in the 'pensions for homemakers' debate in the early 1980s were Louise Dulude and Monica Townson.

12  Such ambiguity was revealed, e.g., in the following exchange between an MP and the president of the CACSW:

> M. Marceau: 'You seem to consider this family allowance system as a salary for women and not for children.'
> Mme Pepin: 'In 1982 ... I am absolutely astounded to hear you say such a thing.'
> M. Marceau: 'No, no! What I meant was ...'
> Mme Pepin: 'It is pay to mothers to be given to the children, for heaven sake!' (Canada, House of Commons Standing Committee on Health, Welfare and Social Affairs, 1982: (CACSW) 52: 54–5).

13  Similar views are expressed in, e.g., Kitchen (1986), and NAC (n.d.).

14  The same observations were also made in, e.g., Rose (1986) and Eichler (1988).

15  David Ross recalled that this measure was narrowly passed by CCSD's board and that a number of members of the board resigned over the decision (personal interview).

16  See, e.g., Canada, House of Commons Legislative Committee on Bill C-70, 1985: (NAC) 4: 30; (Coalition for Family Allowances) 8: 40; (Quebec Voice of Women) 8: 5; and (Saskatchewan Action Committee on the Status of Women) 5: 8.

17  Dulude commented that in 1979 it was politically possible to call for increases to both the Family Allowance and the Child Tax Credit but that by the early 1980s this was no longer the case (Canada, House of Commons Standing Committee on Health, Welfare and Social Affairs, 1982: 51: 16). An alternative interpretation of the events, expressed by one observer, is that NAC did not sufficiently mobilize women to fight for the Family Allowance (Ruth Rose-Lizée, personal interview).

18  The Child Poverty Action Group (CPAG), e.g., which formed in Toronto in 1985–6 and was composed of social agencies and individuals with backgrounds in family and child welfare (e.g., social planning councils), took its cue from U.S. and European groups of the same name. Its main concern

was not poverty per se but rather the decline of support for families with children, of which 'child poverty' was merely a symptom. CPAG was funded by the Laidlaw Foundation, the Children's Aid Society of Metro Toronto, other associations, and through private donations.

19  Namely, Patrick Johnston and Havi Echenberg.

20  Key individuals included, e.g., Terrence Hunsley (then CCSD's director, and previously with the Department of Health and Welfare), David Ross (then CCSD's economist and author of the 'fact books on poverty'), Richard Shillington (a mathematician and statistician then on contract with CCSD), and Ken Battle (then director of NCW).

21  Some of NCW's publications on poverty data include the following: *Measuring Poverty: 1981 Poverty Lines* (1981); *Revised ... Poverty Lines* (1982); *Poverty Lines* (1983), *Poverty in Canada: 1980 – Final Revised Statistics* (1985); *Poverty Lines, Estimates, Poverty Profile* (1988).

22  Ken Battle was also strongly opposed to homemaker pensions, but he was one of the founding members of SPRG.

23  This monthly meeting was regularly attended by about twenty to twenty-five groups (Splane, 1996: 74).

24  The CLC's own proposal for a GAI (presented at its 1988 convention) advocated full employment as the first line of defence against poverty, with a second line provided by social insurance programs, social services, and child benefits to provide for horizontal equity for families, and a progressive tax system. A GAI would be only a final element in the system. The CLC was unable to build an alliance around its position, however, and ultimately dropped the project (Haddow, 1994).

25  John Myles describes this position as the liberal version of the GAI solution; see Myles (1988b).

26  SPRG participants produced the insightful analysis that the Tories altered social policy via a politics of 'stealth,' as discussed earlier, although the analysis presented tended to underscore the changes in the distribution of benefits, rather than in principles, which was also a key element in the transition (Battle, 1993; Gray, 1990; Rice and Prince, 1993).

27  This view is based on my own perception and experience as a researcher on staff at the CACSW during this period.

## 6  Feminism and Child Poverty Discourse in the Late 1980s to Mid-1990s

1  The Liberal Red Book promoted a market-led transition towards the new global economic order, but it also favoured state intervention to guide development (e.g., an active labour market policy to reskill the labour

force). Thus, it reflected a mix of neo-liberal and neo-statist strategies, as defined by Bob Jessop (1993: 28–33).

2 The 1989 budget cut $10 million in grants to advocacy groups (primarily women's, native, and visible minority); $16 million in cuts to advocacy groups, including the Secretary of State Women's Programme and First Nations groups, were announced in the 1990 budget; the 1991 budget announced a $75 million cut to popular sector groups for 1991, and $125 million in 1992 (Cohen, 1997).

3 In 1989 and again in 1990 the Women's Programme of the Department of the Secretary of State had its funding cut by 15%; the 1990 budget announced cuts to three women's magazines, five feminist groups, and eighty women's centres; NAC's core funding was cut by 50% between 1989 and 1992; in 1991 the Court Challenges Programme was dismantled (Vickers, et al., 1993: 22).

4 The Liberal government announced a 5% cut to all advocacy groups in its first budget (February 1994) and suggested the complete withdrawal of government from the business of funding lobby groups (an approach that was supported by the Reform Party; Brodie, 1995: 69). Attacks on the credibility of women's groups were particularly prevalent during the hearings of the 1992 and 1994 Human Resource Development Committee, where groups were frequently queried about who they represented and whether they were really in touch with what 'ordinary' women were concerned with (see, e.g., Canada, House of Commons Legislative Committee on Bill C-80, 1991–2: (NAC) 6: 39; Canada, House of Commons Standing Committee on Human Resource Development, 1994: (NAC) 35: 76; 1994: (Manitoba Women's Coalition on Social Policy) 47: 149; 1994: (REAL Women) 8: 102).

5 This committee was boycotted by opposition MPs and several key social policy groups.

6 In 1990 the Tories increased the number of weeks worked to qualify for UI, reduced the duration of benefits, and imposed heavier penalties on workers who quit their jobs without just cause; in 1993 they reduced UI benefits from 60 to 57% of insurable earnings. Also see McKeen and Porter, 2003.

7 The House of Commons Standing Committee on Human Resources Development held hearings on the 'social security review' in February and March 1994. A discussion paper and several background documents prepared by Lloyd Axworthy, minister of the newly established Department of Human Resources Development (formerly the Departments of Employment and Immigration, and Health and Welfare) established the specific parameters for the second round of hearings held in the fall of

1994. The committee's final report was published in January 1995 (Canada, Standing Committee on Human Resources Development, 1995).

8  HRDC distributed $4.2 million to 165 national, regional, and local non-profit groups to enable them to participate in the process (Banting, 1994: 133).

9  This language had been adopted previously by the Mulroney government in its training initiative announced in April 1989 ('Adjusting to Win'). This approach took the emphasis off so-called passive ('inefficient') measures such as unemployment insurance and placed it on so-called active measures, such as training. It ultimately justified the Conservative withdrawal of the federal contribution to the UI program (Mahon, 1990).

10  The Liberals' 1994 budget announced a tightening of the UI program, reduced benefits, and the shift to a two-tier system. With respect to social transfers to the provinces, the Liberals froze funds to the Canada Assistance Plan and Established Programs Financing (EPF), and then in their 1995 budget, dismantled CAP and EPF and instituted the Canada Health and Social Transfer. The Liberals also proposed (although it was eventually dropped) a significant change to old age pensions with the replacement of the universal Old Age Security and income-tested Guaranteed Income Supplement with a single, income-tested Seniors Benefit (see Battle and Torjman, 1995; Rice, 1995).

11  Dulude's account of the ending of NAC's involvement in SPRG suggests that it was a moment when labour-oriented feminists within NAC gained power over more liberal and moderate feminists: 'When a meeting of SPRG was called while I was past-president, I called Lynn Kaye to say that I was willing to go, but was told that this would not do, even though the issues to be discussed were not controversial. No one else was sent in my place, and as far as I know that was the end of NAC's association with SPRG' (personal interview). The CACSW had left SPRG earlier.

12  NAC's deficit for the year ending March 1994 was more than $60,000 (Bashevkin, 1998: 225).

13  This ambivalence was evident in 1988 when a discussion paper on government programs for parents with young children was rejected by members at NAC's 1988 AGM. According to Louise Dulude, 'The problem was that women who were mostly labour-force oriented could not agree to an expansion of the benefits of women at home. I did not pursue these issues after that' (personal interview).

14  There was also less social tolerance generally for the idea of single mothers staying home to care for their young children, reflecting the socioeconomic

reality that most mothers by this time, even in two-earner households, had to be employed in order to maintain their standard of living.

15 CCSD enhanced its statistical research capabilities with the establishment of the in-house 'Centre for International Statistics on Economic and Social Welfare for Families and Children,' which now generates contract money that accounts for 80% of CCSD's funding. Its contracts are mainly with the federal and provincial government (especially HRDC), and other non-governmental organizations, such as Campaign 2000, the Vanier Institute, the Caledon Institute, United Way, Social Planning Council of Metro Toronto (now called Community Social Planning Council of Toronto), Canadian Child Care Federation, One Voice Seniors Network (Splane, 1996: 122). There has been a continuity from the mid-1980s in the leadership of CCSD: Patrick Johnston, active in SPRG as director of NAPO became director of CCSD in the early 1990s, followed by David Ross, CCSD's key researcher during the 1980s.

16 A contributing factor might have been that NAPO's director Lynn Toupin was evidently held in high esteem by Minister of Finance Paul Martin (personal communication, a social policy advocate, March 1997).

17 According to a former SPRG member, the disbanding of this group (in 1989) reflected the fact that the fear that the Tories would dismantle social programs had dissipated (Terrence Hunsley, personal interview).

18 CPAG became very active in publishing position papers (e.g., CPAG, 1991, 1994a, 1994b).

19 According to CPAG, child poverty increased by one-third between 1980 and 1984 (1986: 1). According to Esping-Andersen, Canada's child poverty growth rate was high compared with European and Scandinavian countries, but modest in comparison with other welfare states undertaking a 'liberal' strategy (i.e., a rise of 3% in the 1980s for two-parent families, as compared with a rise of 10% in the United States and the United Kingdom (1996: 29, footnote 16).

20 By 1994 child poverty organizations were steering clear of the term *universality* and expressing a willingness to settle for a targeted system but one that provided for middle- to low-income parents: 'In 1986, when we came out with our first policy paper, we called for a universal child income credit ... Eight years later there is a different political climate ... What we're prepared to go to bat for is making sure that the incomes and living standards of modest and median-income families are protected, which I would think would be something that this government would support' (Canada, House of Commons Standing Committee on Human Resources

Development, 1994: (CPAG) 33: 53). According to one spokesperson, CPAG was not interested in 'moral victories,' but a genuine improvement in benefits for the poor. By way of contrast, the CLC continued to support the principle of universality in response to the 1994 Green Paper (Canada, House of Commons Standing Committee on Human Resources Development, 1994: (CLC) 32: 22).

21  The 'Group of Seven' was made up of organizations primarily concerned with families and children, including CPAG, the Vanier Institute on the Family, the Family Service Canada, the Canadian Child Welfare Association, the Canadian Council on Children and Youth, and the Canadian Institute of Child Health. It also included longstanding social policy and anti-poverty organizations, such as CCSD. In 1988 this group held a press conference and published a series of fact sheets and a position paper on child poverty (Group of Seven, 1988).

22  A coordinator was hired in 1991 to work half-time for CPAG and half-time for Campaign 2000. CPAG remained a core group behind Campaign 2000, producing most of its analysis.

23  By 1992 the principle of universality was no longer a priority for the Caledon Institute of Social Policy. As Ken Battle told the Legislative Committee on Bill C-80 (which eliminated the family allowance): 'If I have to choose between universality and improving benefits for the poor, I'll choose improving benefits for the poor' (Canada, House of Commons Legislative Committee on Bill C-80, 1991–2: (Caledon) 2: 14). He maintained this position during the 1994 hearings: 'I am much more supportive of selective benefits ... in terms of income security benefits, child benefits, benefits for the elderly, I very much believe in gearing them to need and income' (Canada, House of Commons Standing Committee on Human Resources Development, 1994: (Caledon) 3: 22). This was a departure from the position Battle had taken in 1990 as director of NCW, at which time he had advocated a universal, but targeted child benefits program (NCW, 1990a).

24  These included the 1990 Senate Committee on Social Affairs, Science and Technology, and Sub-Committee on Poverty of the House of Commons Standing Committee on Health, Welfare, Social Affairs, Seniors, and the Status of Women.

25  This idea also had its roots in the views of the Tory 'family caucus,' who had argued that the family allowance was unfair because of its discriminatory effect on single-breadwinner families relative to two-earner families – a situation that the Tories themselves had created in 1989 with the institution of the clawback.

26 For example, child development advocates, such as Dr Fraser Mustard, began to be able to influence the discourse in a way that highlighted the development needs of *young* children (see, e.g., Canada, House of Commons Standing Committee on Human Resources Development, 1994: 49: 22).

27 This observation was also made by Janine Brodie (1996a).

28 NAC and NAWL were the main national women's organizations representing women's interests in these fora. NAC organized a two-day conference on the social security review in Regina in fall of 1994, funded by HRDC, and attended by women's groups from across the country. Some regional groups also mobilized in order to participate in the 1994 social security review hearings (e.g., the Manitoba Women's Coalition on Social Policy).

29 These impressions were gained through personal interviews with individuals who were centrally involved in the debates at this time.

30 Clearly, not all of these groups ignore gender as a variable. For example, CCSD continues to do valuable research on women, and from a feminist perspective.

31 This was pointed out by Therese Jennissen (1996).

32 Status of Women Canada issued a call for proposals in September 1999 that reflected this concern – i.e., 'Where have all the women gone? Changing shifts in policy discourses.'

33 For example, organizations like the Laidlaw Foundation seem to be deploying a discourse on 'social exclusion' mainly as an extension of its focus on children.

## 7 Conclusions

1 Family-based eligibility to UI had been proposed several times previously by the federal government, including in the late 1970s, early 1980s, and mid-1980s. Also see Ann Porter, 2003.

2 A study of the impact of switching from the dependency rate under Unemployment Insurance (which based eligibility on individual earnings) to the family income supplement under Employment Insurance (which is based on family income), shows that 'married' women disproportionately lost entitlement (Phipps et al., 2001).

3 For feminist's reaction to the two-tier structure, also see Canada, House of Commons Standing Committee on Human Resources Development (1994: (NAWL) 11/3/94). On the family-income testing of UI see (ibid., 1994:

(CACSW) 27/10/94; (Manitoba Coalition on Social Policy Development) 26/11/94; (NAC) 8/11/94; and (NAWL) 8/11/94).

4 Workfare refers to shifts in social assistance policy in the 1990s whereby recipients are expected to perform work or participate in work-related requirements as a condition of receiving benefits.

# References

Adams, Ian. 1970. *The Poverty Wall*. Toronto: McClelland and Stewart.

Adams, Ian, William Camerson, Brian Hill, and Peter Penz. 1971. *The Real Poverty Report*. Edmonton: Hurtig.

Arscott, Jane. 1997. 'Draft from Feminism, Gender Analysis and the Federal State in Canada – an Explosive Story Remains Incomplete.' Unpublished paper.

Baetz, Reuban. 1970. 'A GAI: Pie in the Sky or Desirable Objective for the Seventies?' In Allen M. Linden, ed., *Living in the Seventies*. Toronto: Peter Martin Associates, 102–4.

Baker, Maureen, and David Tippen. 1999. *Poverty, Social Assistance, and the Employability of Mothers: Restructuring Welfare States*. Toronto: University of Toronto Press.

Bakker, Isabella. 1996. 'Introduction: The Gendered Foundations of Restructuring in Canada.' In I. Bakker, ed., *Rethinking Restructuring – Gender and Change in Canada*. Toronto: University of Toronto Press, 3–25.

Banting, Keith. 1987a. 'Income Security and Federalism in the 1980s.' In K. Banting, ed., *The Welfare State and Canadian Federalism*. Kingston: McGill-Queen's University Press, 183–214.

1987b. 'The Welfare State and Inequality in the 1980s.' *Canadian Review of Sociology*, 24(3), 309–38.

1994. 'The Way Beavers Build Dams: Social Policy Change in Canada.' In Keith Banting, ed., *A New Social Vision for Canada? Perspectives on the Federal Discussion Paper on Social Security Reform*. Kingston: Caledon Institute of Social Policy and the School of Policy Studies, Queen's University, 131–7.

Banting, Keith, and Ken Battle (eds.). 1994. *A New Social Vision for Canada? Perspectives on the Federal Discussion Paper on Social Security Reform*.

Kingston: Caledon Institute of Social Policy and the School of Policy Studies, Queen's University.

Bashevkin, Sylvia. 1996. 'Losing Common Ground: Feminists, Conservatives and Public Policy in Canada during the Mulroney Years.' *Canadian Journal of Political Science*, 29(2), 205–42.

– 1998. *Women on the Defensive – Living Through Conservative Times*. Toronto: University of Toronto Press.

Battle, Ken. 1993. 'The Politics of Stealth: Child Benefits under the Tories.' In S. Phillips, ed., *How Ottawa Spends, 1993–1994*. Ottawa: Carleton University Press, 417–48.

Battle, Ken and Sherri Torjman. 1995. 'How Finance Re-Formed Social Policy.' In D. Drache and A. Ranachan, eds., *Warm Heart, Cold Country – Fiscal and Social Policy Reform in Canada*. Ottawa and North York: Caledon Institute of Social Policy and Robarts Centre for Canadian Studies, York University, 407–41.

Bhavnani, Kum-Kum, and Margaret Coulson. 1986. 'Transforming Socialist-Feminism: The Challenge of Racism.' *Feminist Review*, 23 (June), 81–93.

Blain, Christine. 1979. 'A Preliminary Review of the Income Tax Act, and Its Implications for an Employment Strategy for Women.' Draft paper, July. Ottawa: Canadian Advisory Council on the Status of Women.

Bleyer, Peter. 1992. 'Coalitions of Social Movements as Agencies for Social Change: The Action Canada Network.' In W. Caroll, ed., *Organizing Dissent – Contemporary Social Movements in Theory and Practice*. Toronto: Garamond Press, 102–17.

Boyd, Monica, Margrit Eichler, and John Hofley. 1976. 'Family: Functions, Formation, and Fertility.' In Gail Cook, ed., *Opportunity for Choice*. Statistics Canada. Ottawa: Information Canada, 16–52.

Brodie, Janine. 1994. 'Shifting the Boundaries: Gender and the Politics of Restructuring.' In Isabella Bakker, ed., *The Strategic Silence – Gender and Economic Policy*. London: Zed Books, 46–60.

– 1995. *Politics on the Margins – Restructuring and the Canadian Women's Movement*. Halifax: Fernwood Publishing.

– 1996a. 'Restructuring and the New Citizenship.' In Isabella Bakker, ed., *Rethinking Restructuring: Gender and Change in Canada*. Toronto: University of Toronto Press, 126–40.

– 1996b. 'Canadian Women, Changing State Forms and Public Policy.' In Janine Brodie, ed., *Women and Canadian Public Policy*. Toronto: Harcourt Brace, 1–28.

– 1998. 'Restructuring and the Politics of Marginalization.' In Manon Tremblay and Caroline Andrew, eds., *Women and Political Representation*. Ottawa: University of Ottawa Press, 19–37.

Brodie, Janine, and Jane Jenson. 1980. *Crisis, Challenge and Change – Party and Class in Canada*. Agincourt: Methuen Publications. 2nd ed., 1989.

Brodie, Janine, Shelley Gavigan, and Jane Jenson. 1992. *The Politics of Abortion*. Toronto: Oxford University Press.

Bryson, Lois. 1983. 'Women as Welfare Recipients: Women, Poverty and the State.' In Cora Baldock and Bettina Cass, ed., *Women, Social Welfare and the State in Australia*. Sydney: George Allen and Unwin, 130–45.

Buchbinder, Howard. 1970. 'Guaranteed Annual Income: The Answer to Poverty for All but the Poor.' *Canadian Dimension*, 7(4), 9–12.

Burt, Sandra. 1994. 'The Women's Movement: Working to Transform Public Life.' In James Bickerton and Alain-G. Gagnon, eds., *Canadian Politics*. Peter-borough: Broadview Press, 207–23.

– 1998. 'The Canadian Advisory Council on the Status of Women: Possibilities and Limitations.' In M. Tremblay and C. Andrew, eds., *Women and Political Representation in Canada*. Ottawa: University of Ottawa Press, 115–44.

Caledon Institute of Social Policy. 1995. *Critical Commentaries on the Social Security Review*. Ottawa: Caledon Institute of Social Policy.

Campaign 2000. 1992. *Countdown 92: Child Poverty Indicator Report*. Prepared by David Hubka, Centre for International Statistics on Economic and Social Welfare for Families and Children at the CCSD, Nov.

– 1994. *Countdown 94: Campaign 2000 Poverty Indicator Report*. Prepared by the Centre for International Statistics on Economic and Social Welfare at the CCSD, Nov.

– 1995. *Child Poverty in Canada, Report Card 1995*. Pamphlet, Campaign 2000, Toronto

Canada, Commission of Inquiry on Unemployment Insurance. 1986. *Report*. Ottawa: Supply and Services Canada, Nov.

– Commission on Equality in Employment. 1984. *Report of the Commission on Equality in Employment*. Oct.

– Department of Finance. 1989. *Budget Papers*. Tabled by the Hon. Michael Wilson, Minister of Finance, 27 April.

– Government of Canada. 1973. *Working Paper on Social Security in Canada*. Ottawa: Minister of National Health and Welfare.

– Health and Welfare Canada. 1992. *Brighter Futures: Canada's Action Plan for Children*.

– House of Commons. 1978. *Debates*.

– Legislative Committee on Bill C-70. 1985. *Minutes of Proceedings and Evidence*. 33rd Parliament, 1st session.

– Legislative Committee on Bill C-80. 1991–2. *Minutes of Proceedings and Evidence*. 34th Parliament, 3rd session.

- Standing Committee on Health, Welfare and Social Affairs. 1982. *Minutes of Proceedings and Evidence*. 32nd Parliament, 1st session.
- 1985. *Minutes of Proceedings and Evidence*. 33rd Parliament, 1st session.
- Seniors, and the Status of Women Subcommittee on Child Poverty. 1991. *Canada's Children: Investing in Our Future*. Dec.
- Standing Committee on Human Resources Development. 1994. *Minutes of Proceedings and Evidence*.
- Human Resources Development Canada (HRDC). 1994. *Agenda: Jobs and Growth – Improving Social Security in Canada: A Discussion Paper*. Oct.
- Minister of Finance. 1984. *A New Direction for Canada: An Agenda for Economic Renewal*. Presented by Michael Wilson, 8 Nov.
- Minister of National Health and Welfare. 1970. *Income Security for Canadians*.
- Minister of National Health and Welfare. 1985. *Child and Elderly Benefits, Consultation Paper*. Jake Epp, Jan.
Canada, Office of the Privy Council, Special Planning Secretariat. 1965. *Meeting Poverty – Profile of Poverty in Canada*.
- 1967. *This Too Is Canada*.
- Parliament, House of Commons. 1992. *Commons Debate*. 34th Parliament, 3rd session, vol. X.
- Parliament, Special Senate Committee on Poverty. 1971. *Poverty in Canada, Report of the Special Senate Committee on Poverty*.
Canada, Royal Commission on the Economic Union and Development Prospects for Canada. 1985. *Report*.
Canada, Royal Commission on the Status of Women (RCSW) 1970. *Report*.
- Senate. 1969. *Proceedings of the Special Senate Committee on Poverty*. No. 7, 18 Nov.
- 1970. *Proceedings of the Special Senate Committee on Poverty*. No. 64, 17 Aug.
- Standing Committee on Health and Welfare, Social Affairs, Seniors and the Status of Women, Sub-committee on Poverty. 1993. *Towards 2000: Eliminating Child Poverty*. Barbara Greene, Chair, June.
- 1991. *Canada's Children: Investing in Our Future*.
Canada, Senate, Standing Committee on Social Affairs, Science and Technology. 1989–90. *Minutes of Proceedings and Evidence*. 34th Parliament, 2nd Session.
- 1992–3. *Minutes of Proceedings and Evidence*. 34th Parliament, 3rd session.
- 1991. *Children in Poverty: Toward a Better Future*.
Canada, Standing Committee on Finance and Economic Affairs. 1987a. *Report on the White Paper on Tax Reform (Stage 1)*. Minutes of Proceedings and Evidence of the Standing Committee on Finance and Economic Affairs. 33rd Parliament, 2nd session. November.

– 1987b. *Minutes of Proceedings and Evidence*. 33rd Parliament, 2nd session.

Canada, Standing Committee on Human Resources Development. 1995. *Security, Opportunities and Fairness: Canadians Renewing Their Social Programs*. Report of the Standing Committee Human Resources Development. Minutes of Proceedings and Evidence of the Standing Committee on Human Resources Development, Issue No. 67. 17 Jan.

Canada, Task Force on Child Care. 1986. *Report of the Task Force on Child Care*.

Canadian Advisory Council on the Status of Women (CACSW). no date. *Women and Aging: A Report on the Rest of Our Lives*. Ottawa: CACSW.

– no date. *Women and Poverty: What Are Your Chances?* Fact sheet no. 6. Ottawa: CACSW.

– 1974. *The Canada Pension Plan and Women – A Discussion Paper*. Prepared by June Menzies. Ottawa: CACSW.

– 1976a. *Background Study on Women and the Personal Income Tax System*. Prepared by Louise Dulude. Ottawa: CACSW.

– 1976b. *New Directions for Public Policy: A Position Paper on the One-Parent Family*. Prepared by June Menzies. Ottawa: CACSW, April.

– 1977a. 'Statements on Taxation.' Ottawa: CACSW, April.

– 1977b. 'Annual Report, 1976–77.' Ottawa: CACSW.

– 1978a. *Annotated Recommendations of the Advisory Council on the Status of Women on the Subject of Women and Taxation*. Ottawa: CACSW.

– 1978b. *Annual Report, 1977–78*. Ottawa: CACSW.

– 1979. *Bill C-6 – An Act to Amend the Old Age Security Act – Recommendations of the CACSW as Submitted to the Standing Committee on Health, Welfare and Social Affairs*. Ottawa: CACSW, Oct.

– 1980a. *Discussion Paper on Federal Income Security Programs for Families with Children*. Ottawa: CACSW.

– 1980b. *Annual Report, 1979–80*. Ottawa: CACSW.

– 1982. *Presentation to the Standing Committee on Health, Welfare and Social Affairs on the Impact on Women of the Proposed Modifications of the Indexing of the Family Allowances and Old Age Pensions*. Ottawa: CACSW, Dec.

– 1984. *Statement on Family Allowances in the Context of the Child Benefits System: A Response by the CACSW to Bill C-70*. Ottawa: CACSW, Nov.

– 1986. *Brief Presented to the Committee of Inquiry on Unemployment Insurance*. Ottawa: CACSW, Jan.

– 1987a. *Background Paper – Women and Income Tax Reform*. Ottawa: CACSW.

– 1987b. *Brief on Tax Reform Presented to the Standing Committee on Finance and Economic Affairs*. Ottawa: CACSW, Dec.

– 1990a. *Women and Labour Market Poverty*. Ottawa: CACSW.

- 1990b. *Women's Poverty Means Child Poverty – A Brief Presented by the CACSW to the Senate Committee on Social Affairs, Science and Technology.* Ottawa: CACSW.

Canadian Association of Social Workers. 1970. 'Brief to the Senate Committee on Poverty.' 24 March.

Canadian Council on Social Development (CCSD). 1971. *The One-Parent Family in Canada.* Ottawa: CCSD.

- 1972. *Guaranteed Annual Income: An Integrated Approach.* Ottawa: CCSD.
- 1973. *Social Security for Canada.* Ottawa: CCSD.
- 1974. *Income Supplements for the Working Poor.* Proceedings of a conference on income supplementation, 8–9 April, 1974, Toronto. Ottawa: CCSD.
- 1975a. *Canadian Fact Book on Poverty.* Prepared by David Ross, Program Director, Income Security. Ottawa: CCSD.
- 1975b. *Proceedings.* Canadian Conference on Social Welfare, 16–20 June, Calgary. Ottawa: CCSD.
- 1976a. *Proceedings.* Canadian Conference on Social Development, 13–17 June, Toronto. Ottawa: CCSD.
- 1976b. *Proceedings.* Conference on Family Income Security Issues. Ottawa: CCSD.
- 1976c. *Women in Need – A Sourcebook.* Ottawa: CCSD.
- 1979a. *The Future of Social Security in Canada.* Ottawa: CCSD.
- 1979b. *Canadian Fact Book on Poverty.* Prepared by Donald Caskie. Ottawa: CCSD.
- 1981. *Social Policies for the Eighties.* Proceedings of the 1980 Canadian Conference on Social Development. St John's, Newfoundland. Ottawa: CCSD, Nov.
- 1983. *Canadian Fact Book on Poverty.* Prepared by David Ross. Toronto: James Lorimer.
- 1984. *Not Enough: The Meaning and Measurement of Poverty in Canada.* Report of the CCSD National Task Force on the Definition and Measurement of Poverty in Canada. Ottawa: CCSD.
- 1985a. 'CCSD Discussion Paper on Social Security.' Draft, Feb.
- 1985b. 'Setting the State.' *Overview,* 2(3), 1.
- 1986a. 'Work and Income in the Nineties, Income Security: Background Information.' *Overview,* 4(1), 5–16.
- 1986b. *The Why, What and How of Income Security Reform.* Work and Income in the Nineties Series. Prepared by David Ross. Ottawa: CCSD.
- 1987. *Work and Income in the Nineties (WIN) Working Paper No. 8, Proposals for Discussion, Phase One – Income Security Reform.* Ottawa: CCSD, Aug.
- 1989. *Canadian Fact Book on Poverty.* Prepared by David Ross and Richard Shillington. Ottawa: CCSD.

- 1994. *The Canadian Fact Book on Poverty – 1994*. Prepared by David Ross, Richard Shillington, and Clarence Lochhead. Ottawa: CCSD.
- 2000. *The Canadian Fact Book on Poverty – 2000*. Prepared by David Ross, Katherine Scott, and Peter Smith. Ottawa: CCSD

Canadian Labour Congress (CLC). 1985. 'Canadian Labour Congress Response to the Standing Committee on Health, Welfare, and Social Affairs.' Brief, March.

Canadian Welfare Council (CWC). 1925. *Problems in Family Desertion*. Presented at the Canadian Conference on Child Welfare, 28 Sept. to 1 Oct. Ottawa: CWC.
- 1941. *Some Problems in Family Maintenance, Desertion, etc. Together with Summaries of Relevant Dominion and Provincial Legislation*. Ottawa: CWC.
- 1956. *Papers on Desertion*. Ottawa: CWC.
- 1961. *Family Desertion – Its Causes and Effects*. Ottawa: CWC, Public Welfare Division.
- 1968. *Study of Family Desertion in Canada*. Prepared for the Royal Commission on the Status of Women. Ottawa: CWC.
- 1969. *Social Policies for Canada, Part I – A Statement by the CWC*. Ottawa: CWC.
- 1970. *Fiftieth Annual Report*. Ottawa: CWC.

Carota, Mario. 1970. *Low Income Interest Groups in Canada*. Ottawa: CWC.

Cass, Bettina. 1994. 'Citizenship, Work, and Welfare: The Dilemma for Australian Women.' *Social Politics*, 1(1), 106–24.

Catholic Women's League of Canada. No date. 'Submission to the Special Senate Committee on Poverty.' National Archives, Ottawa, Special Senate Committee on Poverty file.

Child Poverty Action Group (CPAG). 1986. 'A Fair Chance for All Children: The Declaration on Child Poverty.' Toronto: CPAG, April.
- 1991. 'Unequal Futures: The Legacies of Child Poverty in Canada.' Toronto: CPAG and Social Planning Council of Metropolitan Toronto.
- 1994a. 'Investing in the Next Generation.' Position paper. Toronto: CPAG, July.
- 1994b. 'Perspectives on Public Finance and National Programs.' Position paper, co-produced with Citizens for Public Justice and the Social Planning Council of Metropolitan Toronto. Toronto: CPAG.

Cohen, Marjorie. 1987. 'A Good Idea Goes Bad – Guaranteed Income or Guaranteed Poverty?' *This Magazine*, 21(2), 19–23.
- 1992. 'The Canadian Women's Movement and Its Efforts to Influence the Canadian Economy.' In Constance Backhouse and David Flaherty, eds., *Challenging Times – The Women's Movement in Canada and the United States*. Montreal and Kingston: McGill-Queen's University Press, 215–24.

– 1997. 'From the Welfare State to Vampire Capitalism.' In P. Evans and G.
     Werkerle, eds., *Women and the Canadian Welfare State: Challenges and Change*.
     Toronto: University of Toronto Press, 28–67.
Coleman, William, and Grace Skogstad. 1990. 'Introduction' and 'Policy
     Communities and Policy Networks: A Structural Approach.' In Coleman
     and Skogstad, eds., *Policy Communities and Public Policy in Canada: A Struc-
     tural Approach*. Mississauga: Copp Clark Pitman, 1–13; 14–33.
Collins, Patricia Hill. 1989. 'The Social Construction of Invisibility: Black
     Women's Poverty in Social Problems Discourse.' *Perpsectives on Social
     Problems*, vol. 1, 77–93.
Collins, Kevin. 1978. *Women and Pensions*. Ottawa: Canadian Council on Social
     Development.
Coutts, Jim. 1992. 'Expansion, Retrenchment and Protecting the Future: Social
     Policy in the Trudeau Years.' In T. Axworthy and P.E. Trudeau, eds., *Towards
     a Just Society – The Trudeau Years*. Toronto: Penguin, 221–45.
Dahl, Tove Stang. 1987. *Women's Law – An Introduction to Feminist Jurispru-
     dence*. Oslo: Norwegian University Press.
Daly, Margaret. 1975. 'The Disadvantaged Woman.' In Sheila Arnopoulos,
     Sharon Brown, Dian Cohen, Margaret Daly, Katherine Govier, eds., *To See
     Ourselves – Five Views on Canadian Women*. Ottawa: International Women's
     Year Secretariat, Privy Council Office, 103–23.
Dobrowolsky, Alexandra, and Denis Saint-Martin. 2002. 'Agency, Actors and
     Change in a Child-Focused Future: Problematizing Path Dependency's Past
     and Statist Parameters.' Paper prepared for Canadian Political Science
     Association Meetings, Toronto, University of Toronto, 29 May–1 June.
Dulude, Louise. 1979. 'Taxation of the Family: Joint Taxation of Spouses – A
     Feminist View.' *Canadian Taxation*, 1(4), 8–12.
– 1982. 'Pensions for Housewives – Affirmative.' *Status of Women News*,
     Spring.
Dundas, Jennifer. 1987. 'Economist Warns of Right Wing Support for Annual
     Income.' *Herizons*, Jan.–Feb.
Durst, Douglas. 1999. 'Phoenix or Fizzle? Background to Canada's National
     Child Benefit.' In Douglas Durst, ed., *Canada's National Child Benefit: Phoenix
     or Fizzle?*. Halifax: Fernwood Publishing, 11–37.
Economic Council of Canada (ECC). 1968. *The Challenge of Growth and Change*.
     Fifth annual review. Ottawa: ECC.
– 1992. *The New Face of Poverty – Income Security Needs of Canadian Families*.
     Ottawa: Minister of Supply and Services.
Edwards, Meredith. 1982. 'Families and Taxation.' *Tax Matters Newsletter*, no. 4
     (Jan.) 1–4.

Eichler, Margrit. 1980. '"Family Income" – A Critical Look at the Concept.' *Status of Women*, 6(2), 20–4.

– 1983a. *Families in Canada Today – Recent Changes and Their Policy Consequences.* Toronto: Gage Educational.

– 1983a. 'Women, Families and the State.' In Joan Turner and Lois Emery, eds., *Perspectives on Women in the 1980s.* Winnipeg: University of Manitoba Press, 113–27.

– 1983c. Letter, *Status of Women News*, 8(4), Autumn, 2–3.

– 1988. *Families in Canada Today – Recent Changes and Their Policy Consequences.* Toronto: Gage Educational, 2nd ed.

– 1997. *Family Shifts: Families, Policies, and Gender Equality.* Toronto: Oxford University Press.

Esping-Andersen, Gøsta. 1989. 'The Three Political Economies of the Welfare State.' *Canadian Review of Sociology and Anthropology*, 26(1), 10–36.

– 1990. *The Three Worlds of Welfare Capitalism.* Cambridge: Polity Press.

– 1996. 'After the Golden Age? Welfare State Dilemas in a Global Economy.' In Gøsta Esping-Endersen, ed., *Welfare States in Transition, National Adaptations in Global Economies.* London: Sage, 1–31.

– 1999. *Social Foundations of Postindustrial Economics.* Oxford: Oxford University Press.

Evans, Patricia. 1991. 'The Sexual Division of Poverty: The Consequences of Gendered Caring.' In Carol Baines, Patricial Evans, and Sheila Neysmith, eds., *Women's Caring – Feminist Perspectives on Social Welfare.* Toronto: McClelland and Stewart, 169–203.

– 1996. 'Single Mothers and Ontario's Welfare Policy: Restructuring the Debate.' In Janine Brodie, ed. *Women and Canadian Public Policy.* Toronto: Harcourt Brace and Co.

– 1997. 'Divided Citizenship? Gender, Income Security and the Welfare State.' In P. Evans and G. Wekerle, eds., *Women and the Canadian Welfare State: Challenges and Change.* Toronto: University of Toronto Press, 91–115.

Family Benefits Work Group. Meeting Thursday, 28 Sept. 1978. Canadian Women's Movement Archives, University of Ottawa, Family Benefits Work Group Minutes, Toronto file.

Federal-Provincial Study Group on Alienation. 1971. *Report of the Federal-Provincial Study Group on Alienation to the Federal–Provincial Conference of Ministers of Welfare*, Jan., Ottawa: Department of National Health and Welfare.

Felt, Lawrence. 1978. 'Militant Poor People and the Canadian State.' In Daniel Glenday, Hubert Guidon, and Allan Turowetz, eds., *Modernization and the Canadian State.* Toronto: Macmillan, 417–41.

Finch, Janet. 1990. 'The Politics of Community Care in Britain.' In Clare

Ungerson, ed., *Gender and Caring*. Hemel Hempstead: Harvester Wheatsheaf, 34–58.

Findlay, Peter. 1983. 'Social Welfare in Canada – The Case For Universality.' *Canadian Social Work Review*, 17–24.

Findlay, Suzanne. 1987. 'Facing the State: The Politics of the Women's Movement Reconsidered.' In Heather Jon Maroney and Meg Luxton, eds., *Feminism and Political Economy*. Toronto: Methuen Publications.

– 1988. 'Feminist Struggles with the Canadian State: 1966–1988.' *Resources for Feminist Research*, 17(3), Sept., 5–9.

– 1997. 'Institutionalizing Feminist Politics: Learning from the Struggle for Equal Pay in Ontario.' In Pat Evans and Gerde Wekerle, eds., *Women and the Canadian Welfare State*. Toronto: University of Toronto Press, 310–29.

– 1998. 'Representation and the Struggle for Women's Equality: Issues for Feminist Practice.' In M. Tremblay and C. Andrew, eds., *Women and Political Representation*. Ottawa: University of Ottawa Press.

Ford, George, and Steven Langdon. 1970. 'Just Society Movement – Toronto's Poor Organize.' *Canadian Dimension*, 7(4), 17–21.

Fraser, Nancy. 1994. 'After the Family Wage – Gender Equity and the Welfare State.' *Political Theory*, 22(4), 591–618.

Freiler, Christa, and Judy Cerny. 1998. *Benefiting Canada's Children: Perspectives on Gender and Social Responsibility*. Ottawa: Status of Women Canada.

Freiler, Christa, Felicite Stairs, Brigitte Kitchen, and Judy Cerny. 2001. *Mothers as Earners, Mothers as Carers: Responsibility for Children, Social Policy and the Tax System*. Ottawa: Status of Women Canada.

*Globe and Mail*. 1978. 'Tax Change Could Hurt Women, Tory MP Says.' 30 Nov., T4.

Goldfield, Evelyn, Sue Munaker, and Naomi Weisstein. 1972. 'Why Women's Liberation?' In Bryan Finnigan and Cy Gonick, eds., *Making It: The Canadian Dream*. Toronto: McClelland and Stewart, 557–62.

Gonick, C.W. 1970. 'Poverty and Capitalism.' *Canadian Dimension*, Kit No. 11, 1–8.

Gotell, Lise. 1998. 'A Critical Look at State Discourse on "Violence against Women": Some Implications for Feminist Politics and Women's Citizenship.' In Manon Tremblay and Caroline Andrew, eds., *Women and Political Representation in Canada*. Ottawa: University of Ottawa Press, 39–84.

Gray, Gratton. 1990. 'Social Policy by Stealth.' *Policy Options Politiques*, 11(2), 17–29.

Group of Seven. 1988. *A Choice of Futures: Canada's Commitment to Its Children*. Ottawa, Canadian Council on Social Development, Sept.

Guyatt, Doris. 1971. *One-Parent Family in Canada*. Ottawa: Vanier Institute of the Family.

Haddad, Jane. 1985. 'Sexism and Social Welfare Policy: The Case of Family Benefits in Ontario.' Occasional Papers in Social Policy Analysis, No. 8, Department of Sociology in Education, Ontario Institute for Studies in Education, Toronto.

– 1986. 'Women and the Welfare State: The Introduction of Mothers' Allowance in Ontario in the 1920s.' Master's thesis, Department of Education, University of Toronto.

Haddow, Rodney. 1990. 'The Poverty Policy Community in Canada's Liberal Welfare State.' In William Coleman and Grace Skogstad, eds., *Organized Interests and Public Policy*. Toronto: Copp-Clark, 212–37.

– 1993. *Poverty Reform in Canada, 1958–1978: State and Class Influences on Policy Making*. Montreal and Kingston: McGill-Queen's University Press.

– 1994. 'Canadian Organized Labour and the Guaranteed Annual Income.' In Andrew Johnson, Stephen McBride, and Patrick Smith, eds., *Continuities and Discontinuities: The Political Economy of Social Welfare and Labour Market Policy in Canada*. Toronto: University of Toronto Press, 350–66.

Harmer, Lesley. 1992. 'The Feminization of Poverty.' *Canadian Women's Studies*, 12(4), 6–9.

– 1995. 'Family Poverty and Economic Struggles.' In Nancy Mandell and Ann Duffy, eds., *Canadian Families – Diversity, Conflict and Change*. Toronto: Harcourt Brace, 235–69.

Harp, John, and John R. Hofley. 1971. *Poverty in Canada*. Scarborough: Prentice-Hall.

Head, Wilson. 1969. 'Poverty: A Major Issue Confronting Canadians.' Prepared by members of a Task Force on Poverty for presentation to the Harrison Liberal Conference, 21–3 Nov., Harrison Hot Springs, British Columbia.

Hirschmann, Nancy, and Ulrike Liebert. 2001. *Women and Welfare – Theory and Practice in the United States and Europe*. New Brunswick, NJ, and London: Rutgers University Press.

Hobson, Barbara. 1990. 'No Exit, No Voice: Women's Economic Dependency and the Welfare State.' *Acta Sociologica*, 33(3), 235–50.

– 1994. 'Solo Mothers, Social Policy Regimes and the Logics of Gender.' In Diane Sainsbury, ed., *Gendering Welfare States*. London: Sage. 170–87.

Hunt, Scott, Robert Benford, and David Snow. 1994. 'Identity Fields: Framing Processes and the Social Construction of Movement Identities.' In Enrique Larana, Hank Johnston, and Joseph Gusfield, eds., *New Social Movements, From Ideology to Identity*. Philadelphia: Temple University Press, 185–208.

James, Alice. 1968. 'Brief to the Royal Commission on the Status of Women.' National Archives. Ottawa, RCSW file.

– 1972. 'Poverty: Canada's Legacy to Women.' In *Women Unite!* Discussion Collective. No. 6. (Bonnie Campbell, et al., eds) Toronto: Canadian Women's Educational Press, 125–38.

Jennissen, Therese. 1996. 'The Federal Social Security Review: A Gender-sensitive Critique.' In Jane Pulkingham and Gordon Ternowetsky, eds., *Remaking Canadian Social Policy*. Halifax: Fernwood Publishing, 238–55.

Jenson, Jane. 1986. 'Gender and Reproduction: Or, Babies and the State.' *Studies in Political Economy*, no. 20 (Summer), 9–45.

– 1987. 'Changing Discourse, Changing Agendas: Political Rights and Reproductive Policies in France.' In Mary Fainsod Katzenstein and Carol McClurg Mueller, eds., *The Women's Movements of the United States and Western Europe*. Philadelphia: Temple University Press, 64–88.

– 1990. 'Different but Not Exceptional: The Feminism of Permeable Fordism.' *New Left Review*, Nov./Dec., 58–68.

– 1993. 'Naming Nations: Making Nationalist Claims in Canadian Public Discourse.' *Canadian Review of Sociology and Anthropology*, 30(3), 337–58.

– 1994. 'Understanding Politics: Contested Concepts of Identity in Political Science.' In James Bickerton and Alain-G. Gagnon, eds., *Canadian Politics*, 2nd ed. Peterborough: Broadview Press, 54–74.

– 1995. 'What's in a Name? Nationalist Movements and Public Discourse.' In H. Johnston and B. Klandermans, eds., *Social Movements and Culture*. Minneapolis: University of Minnesota Press, 107–26.

– 1996. 'Part-Time Employment and Women: A Range of Strategies.' In I. Bakker, ed., *Rethinking Restructuring – Gender and Change in Canada*. Toronto: University of Toronto Press, 92–108.

– 1997. 'Who Cares? Gender and Welfare Regimes.' *Social Politics*, 4(2), 182–7.

– 2000. 'Canada's Shifting Citizenship Regime. The Child as "Model Citizen."' Unpublished manuscript.

Jenson, Jane, Rianne Mahon, and Susan Phillips. 2003. 'No Minor Matter: The Political Economy of Child Care in Canada.' In Wallace Clement and Leah Vosko, eds., *Changing Canada: Political Economy as Transformation*. Kingston and Montreal: McGill-Queens University Press.

Jenson, Jane, and Denis Saint-Martin. 2002. 'Working Paper no. 4 – Building Blocks for a New Welfare Architecture: From Ford to LEGO?' Paper prepared for Annual Meeting of American Political Science Association, Boston, 28 Aug. to 1 Sept.

Jenson, Jane, and Susan Phillips. 1996. 'Regime Shift: New Citizenship Practices in Canada.' *International Journal of Canadian Studies*, 14(Fall), 111–36.

Jessop, Bob. 1993. 'Towards a Schumpeterian Workfare State? Preliminary Remarks on Post-Fordist Political Economy.' *Studies in Political Economy*, no. 40 (Spring), 7–39.

Kitchen, Brigitte. 1979. 'A Canadian Compromise: The Refundable Child Tax Credit.' *Canadian Taxation*, 1(3), 44–51.

– 1980. 'Women and the Social Security System in Canada.' *Atlantis*, 5(2), 89–99.

– 1984. 'Women's Dependence.' *Atkinson Review of Canadian Studies*, 1(2), 11–16.

– 1986. 'The Patriarchal Bias of Income Tax in Canada.' *Atlantis*, 11(2), 35–46.

Korpi, Walter. 1989. 'Power, Politics, and State Autonomy in the Development of Social Citizenship.' *American Sociological Review*, 54(3), 309–28.

Kress, Gunther. 1985. *Linguistic Processes in Sociocultural Practice*. Victoria: Deakin University Press.

Land, Hilary. 1979. 'The Boundaries between the State and the Family.' In Chris C. Harris, in association with Michael Anderson, eds., *The Sociology of the Family: New Directions for Britain*. London: Sociological Review Monograph, no. 28. 141–59.

Lang, Lynn. 1972. 'Women on Welfare.' In *Women Unite!* Toronto: Canadian Women's Press, 152–7.

Larner, Wendy. 2000. 'Neo-Liberalism: Policy, Ideology, Governmentality.' *Studies in Political Economy*, 63, Autumn, 5–25.

Leueen. 1971. 'Equal Opportunities but ...' *Pedestal*, 3(1), 9.

Lewis, Jane. 1992. 'Gender and the Development of Welfare Regimes.' *Journal of European Social Policy*, 2(3), 159–73.

– 1997. 'Gender and Welfare Regimes: Further Thoughts.' *Social Politics*, 4(2), Summer, 160–77.

Liberal Party of Canada. 1993. *Creating Opportunity – the Liberal Plan for Canada*. Ottawa: Liberal Party of Canada.

Lister, Ruth. 1990. 'Women, Economic Dependency and Citizenship.' *Journal of Social Policy*, 19(4), 445–67.

– 1995. 'Dilemmas in Engendering Citizenship.' *Economy and Society*, 24(1), 1–40.

Little, Margaret. 1999. 'The Limits of Canadian Democracy: The Citizenship Rights of Poor Women.' *Canadian Review of Social Policy*, 43, 59–76.

Loney, Martin. 1977. 'A Political Economy of Citizen Participation.' In L. Panitch, ed., *The Canadian State: Political Economy and Political Power*, Toronto: University of Toronto Press, 446–72.

Luckhaus, Linda. 1994. 'Individualisation of Social Security Beneifits.' In C. McCrudden, ed., *Equality of Treatment between Women and Men in Social Security*. London: Butterworth, 147–61.

Luxton, Meg. 1997. 'Feminism and Families: The Challenge of Neo-Conservatism.' In M. Luxton, ed., *Feminism and Families – Critical Policies and Changing Practices*. Halifax: Fernwood Publishing, 10–26.

– 2002. 'Feminist Perspectives on Social Inclusion and Children's Well-Being.' A working paper published by the Laidlaw Foundation.

MacDaniel, Susan. 1993. 'The Changing Canadian Family: Women's Roles and the Impact of Feminism.' In S. Burt, L. Code, D. Lindsay, eds., *Changing Patterns – Women in Canada*. Toronto: McClelland and Stewart, 103–27.

MacDonald, Martha. 1998. 'Gender and Social Security Policy: Pitfalls and Possibilities.' *Feminist Economics*, 4(1), 1–25.

Mahon, Rianne. 1990. 'Adjusting to Win? The New Tory Training Initiative.' In K. Graham, ed., *How Ottawa Spends, 1990–91, Tracking the Second Agenda*. Ottawa: Carleton University Press, 73–111.

– 1997a. 'Child Care in Canada and Sweden: Policy and Politics.' *Social Politics*, 4(3), 382–418.

– 1997b. 'The Never-Ending Story Part 1: Feminist Struggle to Reshape Canadian Day-Care Policy in the 1970s.' First draft of a paper presented at the conference on Gender, Citizenship and the Work of Caring, University of Illinois, 14–16 Nov. 1997.

2002. 'Gender and Welfare State Restructuring: Through the Lens of Child Care.' In Rianne Mahon and Sonya Michel, eds., *Child Care Policy at the Crossroads: Gender and Welfare State Restructuring*. New York and London: Routledge, 1–27.

Maioni, Antonia. 1994. 'Ideology and Process in the Politics of Social Reform.' In *A New Social Vision for Canada? Perspectives on the Federal Discussion Paper on Social Security Reform*. Proceedings of a conference held at Queen's University, 17 Oct. 1994. Kingston: School of Policy Studies, Queen's University.

Mandell, Nancy. 1998. 'Silenced and Forgotten Women: Race, Poverty, and Disability.' In Nancy Mandell, ed., *Feminist Issues – Race, Class, and Sexuality*, 2nd ed. Scarborough: Prentice Hall, Allyn and Bacon, 27–54.

Mann, W.E. 1970. *Poverty and Social Policy in Canada*. Toronto: Copp Clark.

Maroney, Heather Jon. 1987. 'Feminism at Work.' In Heather Jon Maroney and Meg Luxton, eds., *Feminism and Political Economy*. Toronto: Methuen, 85–107.

McBride, Stephen, and John Shields. 1993. 'Neo-Conservatism in Canada: Importing a Foreign Model.' In S. McBride and J. Shields, eds., *Canada and the New World Order*. Halifax: Fernwood Publishing, 5–41.

McClain, Janet, and Cassie Doyle. 1984. *Women and Housing*. Ottawa: CCSD.

McCormack, Thelma. 1972. 'Poverty in Canada: The Croll Report and Its Critics.' *Canadian Review of Sociology and Anthropology*, 9(4), 366–72.

McGrath, Susan. 1997. 'Child Poverty Advocacy and the Politics of Influence.' In Jane Pulkingham and Gordon Ternowetsky, eds., *Child and Family Policies, Struggles, Strategies and Options.* Halifax: Fernwood, 172–87.

McIntosh, Mary. 1978. 'The State and the Oppression of Women.' In Annette Kuhn and AnnMarie Wolpe, eds., *Feminism and Materialism.* London: Routledge and Kegan Paul, 254–89.

McKeen, Wendy. 1989. 'Canadian Social Policy and Women: An Assessment of Current Directions in Income Security Proposals.' Unpublished course paper, Department of Sociology and Anthropology, Carleton University, May.

– 1994a. 'The Wages for Housework Campaign: Its Contribution to Feminist Politics in the Area of Social Welfare in Canada.' *Canadian Review of Social Policy*, no. 33 (Spring/Summer), 21–43.

– 1994b. 'The Radical Potential of the European Community's Equality Legislation.' *Studies in Political Economy*, 43 (Spring), 117–36.

– 2001. 'Shifting Policy and Politics of Federal Child Benefits in Canada.' *Social Politics – International Studies in Gender, State, and Society*, Summer, 186–90.

McKeen, Wendy, and Ann Porter. 2003. 'Politics and Transformation: Welfare State Restructuring in Canada.' In Wallace Clement and Leah Vosko, eds., *Changing Canada: Political Economy as Transformation.* Montreal and Kingston: McGill-Queen's University Press, 109–34.

McLaughlin, E., and C. Glendinning. 1994. 'Paying for Care in Europe: Is There a Feminist Approach?' In Linda Hantrais and Steen Mangen, eds., *Family Policy and the Welfare of Women.* Leicestershire: Cross-National Research Group, European Research Centre, Loughborough University of Technology, March, 52–69.

Millar, Jane. 1989. 'Social Security, Equality and Women in the UK.' *Policy and Politics*, 17(4), 311–19.

Millar, Jane, and C. Glendinning. 1987. 'Invisible Women, Invisible Poverty.' In C. Glendinning and J. Millar, eds., *Women and Poverty in Britain.* Brighton: Wheatsheaf Books, 3–27.

The Minus Ones. 1968. 'Brief Concerning Women Alone with Dependent Children.' Brief no. 146.

Molyneux, Maxine. 1985. 'Mobilization without Emancipation? Women's Interests, the State and Revolution in Nicaragua.' *Feminist Studies*, 11, 227–54.

Morton, Peggy. no date. 'They Are Burning, They Are Burning Effigies: Why, Why, Why, Effigies?' Canadian Women's Movement Archives, University of Ottawa, Hogtown Press, Toronto file.

Moscovitch, Allan. 1982. 'Family Allowances or Child Tax Credits?' *Canadian Journal of Social Work Education*, 8(3), 93–7.
– 1990. '"Slowing the Steamroller": The Federal Conservatives, the Social Sector and Child Benefits Reform.' In Katherine Graham, ed., *How Ottawa Spends, 1990–91: Tracking the Second Agenda*. Ottawa: Carleton University Press, 171–217.
– 1996. 'Canada Health and Social Transfer: What Was Lost?' *Canadian Review of Social Policy*, no. 37 (Spring), 66–75.
Mosher, Janet. 2000. 'Managing the Disentitlement of Women: Glorified Markets, the Idealized Family, and the Undeserving Other.' In Sheila Neysmith, ed., *Restructuring Caring Labour: Discourse, State Practice, and Everyday Life*. Don Mills: Oxford University Press, 30–51.
Mother-Led Union. No date. 'Brief on Financial Independence for Single Support Mothers.' Canadian Women's Movement Archives, University of Ottawa, Mother-Led Union, Toronto file.
Mother's Action Group. 1982. *Protecting Our Own*. Canadian Women's Movement Archives, University of Ottawa, Mother's Action Group, Toronto file.
Mothers on Social Allowance of Metro Winnipeg. 1969. 'Mothers' Committee Brief on Social Allowance.' 10 Nov.
Myles, John. 1988a. 'Social Policy in Canada.' In E. Rathbone-McCuan and B. Havens, eds., *North American Elders, United States and Canadian Perspectives*. New York: Greenwood Press, 37–53.
– 1988b. 'Decline or Impasse? The Current State of the Welfare State.' *Studies in Political Economy*, 26 (Summer), 73–107.
– 1996. 'When Markets Fail: Social Welfare in Canada and the United States.' In G. Esping-Andersen, ed., *Welfare States in Transition*. London: Sage. 116–40.
Myles, John, and Paul Pierson. 1997. 'Friedman's Revenge: The Reform of "Liberal" Welfare States in Canada and the United States.' *Politics and Society*, 25(4), 443–72.
National Action Committee on the Status of Women (NAC). No date. 'Presentation to Sub-Committee on Equality Rights, Standing Committee on Justice and Legal Affairs.' Unpublished brief, June.
– 1978a. Presentation to Cabinet, 17 March. Canadian Women's Movement Archives, University of Ottawa, NAC Briefs, Miscellaneous file.
– 1978b. Brief to the House of Commons Standing Committee on Labour, Manpower and Immigration (Bill C-14). Toronto: NAC.
– 1981. *Women and Pensions*. Discussion Paper, National Pension Conference, Ottawa, 31 March. Toronto: NAC.
– 1982. 'Women and Pensions.' Toronto: NAC, Sept.

– 1983. *Pension Reform – What Women Want.* Toronto: NAC, March.

– 1986. 'The Problem Is Jobs ... Not Unemployment Insurance.' A brief to the Committee of Inquiry on Unemployment Insurance, Toronto: NAC, 28 Jan.

– 1987. *Brief on Tax Reform.* Presented to the House of Commons Standing Committee on Finance and Economic Affairs. Toronto: NAC, Nov.

National Anti-Poverty Organization (NAPO). 1985. *Child and Elderly Benefits.* Ottawa: NAPO, March.

National Council of Welfare (NCW). 1971. *Statement on Income Security.* Ottawa: NCW.

– 1972. '... And a View from the National Council of Welfare.' *Canadian Welfare,* 48(1), 3, 28, 29.

– 1973. *Incomes and Opportunities.* Ottawa: NCW.

– 1975. *Poor Kids.* Ottawa: NCW, March.

– 1976a. *Guide to a Guaranteed Income.* Ottawa: NCW.

– 1976b. *One in a World of Twos, a Report of the NCW on One-Parent Families in Canada.* Ottawa: NCW.

– 1978. *Bearing the Burden, Sharing the Cost.* Ottawa: NCW.

– 1979a. *Women and Poverty,.* Ottawa: NCW.

– 1979b. *In the Best Interests of the Child.* Ottawa: NCW.

– 1981. *Measuring Poverty: 1981 Poverty Lines.* Ottawa: NCW.

– 1982. *Revised Poverty Lines.* Ottawa: NCW.

– 1983. *Family Allowances for All?* Ottawa: Minister or Supply and Services.

– 1985. *Opportunity for Reform. A Response to the Consultation Paper on Child and Elderly Benefits.* Ottawa: NCW, March.

– 1986a. *The Impact of the 1985 and 1986 Budgets on Disposable Income.* Ottawa: Minister of Supply and Services, April.

– 1986b. *Progress Against Poverty.* Ottawa: NCW, Oct.

– 1988. *Poverty Lines, Estimates, Poverty Profile.* Ottawa: NCW.

– 1990a. *Fighting Child Poverty.* Ottawa: NCW.

– 1990b. *Women and Poverty Revisited.* Ottawa: NCW.

Nelson, Barbara. 1984. 'Women's Poverty and Women's Citizenship: Some Political Consequences of Economic Marginality.' *Signs,* 10(2), 209–31.

– 1990. 'The Origins of the Two-Channel Welfare State: Workmen's Compensation and Mothers' Aid.' In Linda Gordon, ed., *Women, the State and Welfare.* Madison: University of Wisconsin Press, 123–51.

Newfoundland Royal Commission on Employment and Unemployment. 1986. *Building on Our Strengths.* St John's.

O'Connor, Julia. 1993. 'Gender, Class and Citizneship in the Comparative Analysis of Welfare State Regimes: Theoretical and Methodological Issues.' *British Journal of Sociology,* 44(3), 501–18.

– 1996. *From Women in the Welfare State to Gendering Welfare State Regimes.* Trend Report. Special issue of *Current Sociology*, 44(2).

– O'Connor, Julia, Ann Shola Orloff, and Sheila Shaver. 1999. *States, Markets, Families: Gender, Liberalism and Social Policy in Australia, Canada, Great Britain, and the United States.* Cambridge: Cambridge University Press.

Ontario, Advisory Group on New Social Assistance Legislation. 1992. *Time for Action – Towards a New Social Assistance System for Ontario.* Toronto: Queen's Printer for Ontario, May.

– Fair Tax Commission. 1992. 'Women and Taxation – Working Group Report.' Nov.

– Social Assistance Review Committee. 1988. *Transitions.* Toronto: Queen's Printer for Ontario.

Orloff, Anne Shola. 1993. 'Gender and the Social Rights of Citizenship: The Comparative Analysis of Gender Relations and Welfare States.' *American Sociological Review*, 53(3), 303–28.

– 1997. 'Comment on Jane Lewis's "Gender and Welfare Regimes": Further Thoughts.' *Social Politics*, 4(2), Summer, 188–202.

Ostner, Ilona, and Jane Lewis. 1995. 'Gender and the Evolution of European Social Policies.' In Stephan Leibfried and Paul Pierson, eds., *European Social Policy.* Washington: Brookings Institute, 159–93.

Pahl, J. 1989. *Money and Marriage.* London: Macmillan.

Pal, Leslie. 1993. *Interests of State – The Politics of Language, Multiculturalism, and Feminism in Canada.* Kingston: McGill-Queen's University Press.

Pascal, Gillian. 1993. 'Citizenship – A Feminist Analysis.' In Glenn Drover and Eric Kerans, eds., *New Approaches to Welfare Theory.* Aldershot: Edward Elgar, 113–26.

*The Pedestal.* 1971. 'Pie in the Sky,' 3(1), 8.

Phillips, Susan. 1990. 'Projects, Pressure and Perceptions of Effectiveness: Organizational Analysis of National Women's Groups.' Unpublished doctoral dissertation.' Carleton Unviversity, Ottawa.

– 1991. 'How Ottawa Blends: Shifting Government Relationships with Interest Groups.' In F. Abele, ed., *How Ottawa Spends, The Politics of Fragmentation, 1991–92.* Ottawa: Carleton University Press, 183–22.

– 1994a. 'Making Change: The Potential for Innovation under the Liberals.' In Susan Phillips, ed., *How Ottawa Spends 1994–95: Making Change.* Ottawa: Carleton University Press, 1–37.

– 1994b. 'New Social Movements in Canadian Politics: On Fighting and Starting Fires.' In J. Bickerton, A-G Gagnon, eds., *Canadian Politics*, 2nd ed. Peterborough: Broadview Press, 188–206.

– 1996. 'Discourse, Identity, and Voice: Feminists Contributions to Policy Studies.' In L. Dobuzinskis, M. Howlett, and D. Laycock, eds., *Policy Studies in Canada: The State of the Art*. Toronto: University of Toronto Press, 242–65.

- 2001. 'SUFA and Citizen Engagement: Fake or Genuine Masterpiece?' *Policy Matters* 2(7), 1–36.

Phipps, Shelley, and P. Burton. 1996. 'The Impact of Employment Insurance on New-Entrant and Re-entrant Workers.' Final Report. Prepared for Human Resources Development Canada, Strategic Evaluation and Monitoring Directorate.

Phipps, Shelley, Martha MacDonald, and Fiona MacPhail. 2001. 'Gender Equity within Families versus Better Targeting: An Assessment of the Family Income Supplement to Employment Insurance Benefits.' *Canadian Public Policy*, 27(4), 423–46.

Pierson, Paul. 1996. 'The New Politics of the Welfare State.' *World Politics*, 48, 143–79.

Podoluk, Jenny R. 1968. *Incomes of Canadians*. Ottawa: Queen's Printer.

Popham, Rosemarie, David Hay, and Colin Hughes. 1997. 'Campaign 2000 to End Child Poverty: Building and Sustaining a Movement.' In B. Wharf and M. Clague, eds., *Community Organizing – Canadian Experiences*. Toronto: Oxford University Press, 248–72.

Porter, Ann. 2003. *Gendered States: Women, Unemployment Insurance, and the Political Economy of the Welfare State in Canada, 1945–1997*. Toronto: University of Toronto Press.

- 1999. 'Family, Labour Markets and the State: Dimensions of Welfare State Restructuring.' Unpublished paper. Presented to the Canadian Political Science Association, Sherbrooke, Quebec, 6 June.

Power, Doris. 1972. 'Statement to the Abortion Caravan.' In *Women Unite!* Toronto: Canadian Women's Educational Press. 121–4

Prince, Michael. 1984. 'What Ever Happened to Compassion? Liberal Social Policy 1980–84.' In A. Maslove, ed., *How Ottawa Spends 1984: The New Agenda*. Toronto: Methuen, 79–121.

Pringle, Rosemary, and Sophie Watson. 1990. 'Fathers, Brothers, Mates: The Fraternal State in Australia.' In Sophie Watson, ed., *Playing the State – Australian Feminist Interventions*. London: Verso, 229–43.

- 1992. '"Women's Interests" and the Post-Structuralist State.' In Michelle Barrett and Anne Phillips, eds., *Destabilizing Theory*. Cambridge: Polity Press, 53–73.

Pross, Paul. 1986. *Group Politics and Public Policy*. Toronto: Oxford University Press. 2nd ed. 1992.

Provincial Council of Women. 1970. 'Brief to the Special Senate Committee on Poverty.' June.

Pulkingham, Jane. 1998. 'Remaking the Social Divisions of Welfare: Gender,

'Dependency,' and UI Reform.' *Studies in Political Economy*, no. 56 (Summer), 7–48.

Pulkingham, Jane, and Gordon Ternowetsky. 1999. 'Child Poverty and the CCTB/NCB: Why Most Poor Children Gain Nothing.' In Doug Durst, ed., *Canada's National Child Benefit: Phoenix or Fizzle?* Halifax: Fernwood Publishing, 103–23.

Quadagno, Jill. 1990. 'Race, Class, and Gender in the U.S. Welfare State: Nixon's Failed Family Assistance Plan.' *American Sociological Review*, 55(1), 11–28.

Rebick, Judy. 2000. *Imagine Democracy*. Toronto: Stoddart Publishing.

Rice, James. 1985. 'Politics of Income Security – Historical Developments and Limits to Future Change.' In B. Doern, ed., *The Politics of Economic Policy*. Toronto: University of Toronto Press in co-operation with the Royal Commission on the Economic Union and Development Prospects for Canada, 221–50.

– 1989. 'Restitching the Safety Net: Altering the National Social Security System.' In Michael J. Prince, ed., *How Ottawa Spends, 1987–88: Restraining the State*. Toronto: Methuen, 211–36.

Rice, James and Michael Prince. 1981. 'The Department of National Health and Welfare: The Attack on Social Policy.' In B. Doern, ed., *How Ottawa Spends Your Tax Dollars – Federal Priorities*. Toronto: James Lorimer, 90–119.

– 1993. 'Lowering the Safety Net and Weakening the Bonds of Nationhood: Social Policy in the Mulroney Years.' In Susan Phillips, ed., *How Ottawa Spends, 1993–1994*. Ottawa: Carleton University Press, 381–416.

– 1995. 'Redesigning Welfare: The Abandonment of a National Commitment.' In Susan Phillips, ed., *How Ottawa Spends, 1995–96; Mid-Life Crisis*. Ottawa: Carleton University Press, 185–207.

Robinson, Claude K. 1967. 'Poverty Canada: Profile and Prescription.' Thesis, Bachelor of Journalism, Carleton University.

Rose, Ruth. 1986. 'Demystifying the Notion of a Guaranteed Minimum Income.' Unpublished paper, Department of Economics, University of Quebec at Montreal, June.

Ross, David. 1985. 'The Great Universality Debate: What Was It all About?' *Perception*, 8(3), 5–8.

– 1986a. 'Plight of the Poor.' *Facts*, 8(2), 41–6.

– 1986b. 'The Macdonald Commission and the Poor.' *Perception*, 9(3), 10–13.

Ruggie, Mary. 1984. *The State and Working Women: A Comparative Study of Britain and Sweden*. Princeton: Princeton University Press.

Sainsbury, Diane. 1994. 'Women's and Men's Social Rights: Gendering Dimensions of Welfare States.' In D. Sainsbury, ed., *Gendering Welfare States*. London: Sage, 150–69.

– 1996. *Gender, Equality and Welfare States*. Cambridge: Cambridge University Press.

Sapiro, Virginia. 1990. 'The Gender Basis of Amercian Social Policy.' In Linda Gordon, ed., *Women, the State and Welfare*. Madison: University of Wisconsin Press, 36–54.

Sarlo, Christopher. 1992. *Poverty in Canada*. Vancouver: Fraser Institute.

Schlesinger, Benjamin. 1969. *The One-Parent Family*. Toronto: University of Toronto Press. Revised 1970 and 1978.

– 1970. 'Families of Misfortune.' In W.E. Mann, ed., *Poverty and Social Policy in Canada*. Toronto: Copp Clark.

– 1972. *What about Poverty in Canada?* Toronto: Guidance Centre, Faculty of Education, University of Toronto.

– 1979. *One in Ten – The Single Parent in Canada*. Toronto: Guidance Centre, Faculty of Education, University of Toronto.

Scott, Katherine. 1996. 'The Dilemma of Liberal Citizenship: Women and Social Assistance Reform in the 1990s.' *Studies in Political Economy*, no. 50, 7–36.

Shaver, Sheila. 1989. 'Gender, Class and the Welfare State: The Case of Income Security in Australia.' *Feminist Review*, no. 32, 90–110.

Shifrin, Leonard. 1978. 'Is There a Commitment to a New Approach to Income Redistribution?' In *Canadian Conference on Social Development, 1978, Proceedings*. Ottawa: CCSD, 177–81.

– 1978b. 'Remarks on Universal vs Selective Income Security and Service Delivery.' In *Canadian Conference on Social Development, 1978, Proceedings*. Ottawa: CCSD, 91–8.

– 1978c. 'Building the Missing Bridge.' *Perception*, Nov.–Dec., 12.

– 1980. 'The Meaninglessness of the Selectivity versus Universality Debate.' *Canadian Taxation*, 2(3), 170–1.

Smith, Miriam. 1992. 'The Canadian Labour Congress: From Continentalism to Economic Nationalism.' *Studies in Political Economy*, no. 38 (Summer), 35–60.

Snow, David, and Robert Benford. 1992. 'Master Frames and Cycles of Protest.' In A. Morris and C. McClurg Mueller, eds., *Frontiers in Social Movement Theory*. New Haven: Yale University, 133–55.

Social Planning Council of Metropolitan Toronto. 1985. 'The Rise and Fall of the Welfare State.' In D. Drache and D. Cameron, eds., *The Other Macdonald Report*. Toronto: James Lorimer, 51–62.

Social Policy Reform Group (SPRG). 1985a. 'Major Social Organizations Back Child Benefit Reform.' Press Release, 31 Jan.
- 1985b. *The Next Budget: What Will It Do for the Poor?* Brief, Dec.
- 1985c. 'The Social Policy Reform Group Response to the Budget.' Draft brief, May.
- 1986. *SPRG Response to the February 1986 Budget.* Brief, Ottawa, February.
Sole Support Parents Coalition. 1982. 'Newsletter.' Unpublished, Canadian Women's Movement Archives, University of Ottawa, Sole Support Parents Coalition, Toronto file.
Spark, Bobbi. 1971. 'An open letter.' *The Pedestal*, 3(6), 5.
Splane, Richard. 1996. *Canadian Council on Social Development, 1920–1995.* Ottawa: CCSD.
Status of Women Canada. 1986. *The Report of the Task Force on Child Care.* Ottawa: Supply and Services.
*Status of Women News.* 1976. 'Resolutions,' 3(1), July.
- 1977. 'Resolutions,' 3(4), May.
- 1978. 'Resolutions,' 4(4), June.
- 1980. 'Resolutions,' 6(3), Summer.
- 1985. 'The Universality Con,' 3 March, 2.
Stroick, Sharon, and Jane Jenson. 1999. *What Is the Best Policy Mix for Canada's Young Children?* Study no. F-09. Ottawa: Canadian Policy Research Network.
*Studies in Political Economy.* 1994. 'Interview with Judy Rebick.' no. 44, Summer, 39–71.
Swift, Karen, and Michael Birmingham. 1999. Caring in a Globalizing Economy. Single Mothers on Assistance.' In Doug Durst, ed., *Canada's National Child Benefit: Phoenix or Fizzle?* Halifax: Fernwood, 84–112.
Townson, Monica. 1980. 'Riding a Treadmill to Poverty.' *Canadian Business Review*, 7(1), 22–9.
- 2000. *A Report Card on Women and Poverty.* Ottawa: Canadian Centre for Policy Alternatives, April.
The Unemployed Citizens' Welfare Improvement Council. 1970. Brief Submitted to the Senate Commission on Poverty. National Archives, Ottawa, Special Senate Committee on Poverty file.
Ursel, Jane. 1992. *Private Lives, Public Policy – 100 Years of State Intervention in the Family.* Toronto: Women's Press.
Van Loon, Richard. 1986. 'Background Document on Income Security.' Working Paper No. 2, Work and Income in the Nineties. Ottawa: CCSD, June.
Vickers, Jill. 1991. 'Bending the Iron Law of Oligarchy – Debates on the Feminization of Organizations and Political Process in the English Canadian

Women's Movement, 1970–1988.' In Jeri Dawn Wine and Janice Ristock, eds., *Women and Social Change: Feminist Activism in Canada*. Toronto: James Lorimer, 75–94.

Vickers, Jill, Pauline Rankin, and Christine Appelle. 1993. *Politics as If Women Mattered: A Political Analysis of the National Action Committee on the Status of Women*. Toronto: University of Toronto Press.

Vosko, Leah. 2000. 'Mandatory "Marriage" or Obligatory Waged Work: Social Assistance and the Single Mother's Complex Roles in Wisconsin and Ontario.' Draft Paper, April.

Walby, Sylvia. 1994. 'Is Citizenship Gendered?' *Sociology*, 28(2), 379–95.

Walker, David. 1971. 'The Poor People's Conference – A Study of the Relationship between the Federal Government and Low Income Interest Groups in Canada.' Master's thesis, Department of Political Studies, Queen's University.

Walker, Gillian. 1990a. 'The Conceptual Politics of Struggle: Wife Battering, the Women's Movement and the State.' *Studies in Political Economy*, 33, Autumn, 63–90.

– 1990b. *Family Violence and the Women's Movement: The Conceptual Politics of Struggle*. Toronto: University of Toronto Press.

Wiegers, Wanda. 2002. *The Framing of Poverty as 'Child Poverty' and Its Implications for Women*. Ottawa: Status of Women Canada.

Wilson, Elizabeth. 1977. *Women and the Welfare State*. London: Tavistock Publications.

Winkler, Celia. 1998. 'Mothering, Equality and the Individual: Feminist Debates and Welfare Policies in the USA and Sweden.' *Community, Work and Family*, 1(2), 149–66.

Winnipeg Welfare Rights Movement. 1970. 'Brief to the Special Senate Committee on Poverty,' Jan.

Wolfson, Michael. 1986. 'A Guaranteed Income.' *Policy Options Politiques*, 7(1), 35–45.

Yeatman, Anna. 1990. *Bureaucrats, Technocrats, Femocrats: Essays on the Contemporary Australian State*. Sydney: Allen and Unwin.

York, Geoffrey. 1992. 'Scrapping Baby Bonuses Seen as Fostering Wife Abuse.' *Globe and Mail*, 15 July, A6.

Zuker, Marvin, and June Callwood. 1971. *Canadian Women and the Law*. Toronto: Copp Clark.

# Index

## Studies in Comparative Political Economy and Public Policy